3000 800024 63218
St. Louis Community College

FV_

WITHDRAWN

 St. Louis Community College

Forest Park
Florissant Valley
Meramec

Instructional Resources
St. Louis, Missouri

GAYLORD

D1088955

The Costume Accessories Series

Socks & Stockings

Jeremy Farrell   General Editor: Dr Aileen Ribeiro

B. T. Batsford Limited, London

LIBRARY
ST. LOUIS COMMUNITY COLLEGE
AT FLORISSANT VALLEY

Contents

To A.E.S

© Jeremy Farrell 1992
First published 1992

All rights reserved. No part of this publication may be reproduced, in any form or by any means, without permission from the publishers.

ISBN 0 7134 6665 0

Typeset by Lasertext Ltd, Stretford, Manchester and printed in Great Britain by Butler and Tanner, Frome, Somerset

for the Publishers
B T Batsford Ltd
4 Fitzhardinge Street London W1H 0AH

A CIP catalogue record for this book is available from the British Library

List of illustrations

Introduction

'One gets the greatest joy of all out of really lovely stockings', said Ursula.
'One does', replied Gudrun; 'the greatest joy of all.'

D H Lawrence   *Women in Love*

Stockings and socks have rarely enjoyed the limelight. Because they could not be taken off easily, they never acquired the chivalric and almost mystical connotations of the hat, the glove, or even the shoe. The garter, rather than the fallen stocking, inspired the origin of the oldest order of chivalry. Their context, instead, has been domestic; the old stockings hung up for Father Christmas to fill with presents, the darned socks, the expression of a woman's love in pre-feminist, pre-disposal days, even the miser's stocking with its hoard of gold hidden under the floorboards. The domestic aura has devalued both the stocking and the sock, just as machine-made mass production has devalued the skills of spinning and knitting, both hand and machine, which made the hosiery of the past possible.

A person of today, accustomed to sheer nylon stockings, would think that there was nothing particularly remarkable in a sheer silk stocking of the kind made for Queen Victoria in the 1840s, or buried beneath the foundation stones of buildings in Nottingham as representative of great mechanical skill, until, that is, that person realised that the expertise of the framework knitter kept each individual row even as it was knitted, and there might be over 2,000 rows in such a stocking, and that the skill of the frame-smith kept the beards of the needles flexible and true. In its way, the nylon stocking which might be discarded after very few wearings is equally remarkable. Twenty-seven miles of nylon filament might go into the making of one stocking. In appearance it might be just a short, narrow bag, but in wear it stretches and clings, flattering the contours of the leg in a way that were it not seen every day would be considered remarkable. The humble sock shares these attributes but has to fight against prejudice which considers it redolent of sports fields and changing rooms, whereas the stocking suggests luxury, glamour and bedrooms. The stocking is sexy, the sock is not. Yet the sock could be made of hand embroidered silk, luxurious to the touch, and not all stockings were wisps of loveliness by any means.

If there are intentions behind this book, other than a straightforward history of socks and stockings, then one of these must surely be an attempt to dispel such prejudice by considering them as products of skill and inventiveness, worthy of reappraisal, and in this way to pay tribute to all the anonymous men and women who made the beautiful hosiery which survives in museum collections. Another must be to throw the spotlight rather more on the product than on the industry, for although the bibliography on hosiery is extensive, it is mostly technical or industrial. The fashionable stocking and sock have altered very little in shape in centuries, but in use, material and decoration they have changed considerably. This book is an attempt to chart some of these changes.

Money and Measurements

Before decimalisation in 1971 there were twenty shillings (s) to every English pound (£) and twelve pence (d) to every shilling. Monetary amounts were written with the pound first followed by shillings and pence (£ s d). After decimalisation there were a hundred new pence (p) to the pound (£). One new penny was roughly equivalent to 2.4 old ones. It is difficult, if not impossible, to make meaningful comparisons of prices today with those of a hundred or more years back. Not only has increasing inflation had an impact but what people spent their income upon and the various proportions of the family budget that were spent on clothes, food, taxes, travel and so forth have radically altered. According to Dr Harold Priestley in *The What It Cost the Day Before Yesterday Book, from 1850 to the present day* (Kenneth Mason, 1979) the successor to an agricultural labourer earning 15s (75p) a week in 1850 might expect to earn £43.00 a week in 1978. Such a sum would be considerably more now. Whenever possible the price of socks and stockings in this book has been linked to the price of clothes at the same period, or a range, from the cheapest to the most expensive, has been given to give some idea of comparability.

Most socks and stockings mentioned in this book were made according to imperial measurements (feet and inches). For quick conversion four inches is roughly equivalent to ten centimetres, one foot (twelve inches) to 30.5 centimetres and three feet to 91.5 centimetres.

Acknowledgements

The research and preparation for this book have been made immeasurably easier by the help and patience of my colleagues and their staff in other museums. I thank particularly: Penelope Byrde at the Fashion Research Centre (the Museum of Costume was regrettably closed for much of this period); Anthea Jarvis and Miles Lambert at the Gallery of English Costume, Manchester; Jill Spanner at the Museum of London; Philip Warren at the Newarke Houses Museum, Leicester; Pamela Wood, Haidee Jackson and Sara Hilton at Newstead Abbey; Diane Moss at Pickford's House Museum, Derby; Maggie Heath at the Ruddington Framework Knitters' Trust: Avril Hart at the Victoria and Albert Museum, and Tina Levey, formerly Keeper of Textiles at the same museum. I am indebted to Avril Hart, to Joanna Marschner of the Court Dress Collection, Kensington Palace, and David Williams of Pretty Polly Ltd for bringing unpublished material to my attention. I am grateful to the Earl of Rosse, the Hon. Michael Willoughby and to Aristoc for permission to use material from their collections, and to Mr Smurfit of HATRA, Samantha Turner of Viyella, Caroline Rees, Elizabeth Dawson and Gwen Davies for help in various ways. I thank Pauline Snelson and Thelma Nye, my editors at Batsford, for their patience, and Dr Aileen Ribeiro for her helpful comments. I am very grateful to Dr Stanley Chapman of Nottingham University for first drawing the J R Allen collection to my attention and to Peta Lewis for her comments on it. The various photographers who have captured so well the fine and fragile nature of hosiery have earned my admiration as well as my thanks. To Dr David Taylor, who has interpreted my handwriting, corrected my grammar, queried my obscurities and who was always ready to discuss knotty problems of interpretation or fact, I am, as always, especially grateful.

J.F.

1
1600–70

William Lee and the stocking frame

Sadly for the historians of hosiery the Elizabethans were not particularly interested in inventors or their inventions. William Lee, the inventor of the stocking frame and father of the hosiery industry, is referred to directly in only five contemporary documents and indirectly in only three more.[1] Not even the concentrated attention which surrounded the quatercentenary, in 1989, of the traditional date of the invention of the stocking frame led to anything new being discovered about him. Little is actually known about him or his invention.

According to tradition, coloured by imagination, he was a native of Woodborough, near Nottingham, a graduate of Cambridge University and a curate at Calverton, also near Nottingham. The inspiration for the invention was either the knitting his fiancée chose to do rather than entertain him, or the knitting his wife had to do to make ends meet. Again, according to the same tradition, he demonstrated his frame to Queen Elizabeth I who declared herself disappointed with the coarse results and refused to grant him a patent. He emigrated to try his luck in France and died of a broken heart in Paris in 1610.[2]

That he is not a mythical figure is proved by the partnership agreement between himself and

1 *Front and back of the stocking frame, drawn by Thomas Sandby, engraved by J Clee for Deering's Nottingham Old and New, 1750*

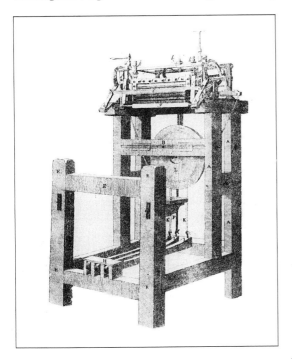
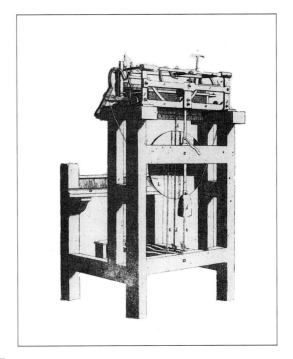

George Brooke, dated 6 June 1600. For an investment of £500 Brooke was to share in development and profits of Lee's 'new artificiality or invention of knitting works'.[3] Lee claimed to be Master of Arts in a petition to the Court of Aldermen of the City of London in 1605, and was still trying to get his machine established in London in 1609. By 1612 he was in Rouen. He had agreed to supply eight machines and six Englishmen to operate them, and to teach French apprentices how to knit by machine. In 1615 he and two other Englishmen were still making stockings in Rouen. Thereafter he fades from history.

But by his own account (in the 1600 partnership agreement) he had by long study and practice 'devised and invented a certain invention or artificiality being a very speedy manner of working and making in a loom or frame all manner of works usually wrought by knitting needles as stockings, waistcoats and such like . . .' He abandoned knitting in the round for knitting in the flat. Instead of a pair of knitting needles he used a row of needles, securing one end of each needle into the frame and bending the point into an open loop which could be closed by a presser bar. Sinkers between the needles forced the thread into loops and the stitches were formed by the presser bar on the beards of the needles. Eric Pasold demonstrated by a model, which is now in the Science Museum, London, how simple Lee's first machine could have been.[4] It did not, however, bring fame and fortune.

Hand knitting

Knitting by machine arose from a background of knitting by hand. The origins of knitting, like many of the textile arts, are unknown and its spread uncharted. It now seems to have developed between AD 500 and 1200 from nalbinding, a looped stitch made with a conventional needle, and to have spread outwards from Egypt by means of trade or conquest.[5] By the thirteenth century it was well established in Spain. Two knitted silk cushions which survive from Spanish tombs of this period have complex

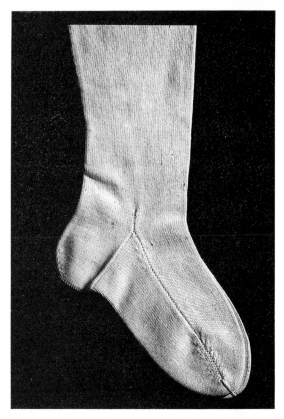

2   Re-creation in white cotton of William Lee's first stocking, made by Allen & Solly and shown at the Great Exhibition, 1851. Length 25½ inches, foot length 11 inches, 11 stitches per inch, 15 rows per vertical inch

patterns of eagles, fleur-de-lys or castles and flowerheads within lattice or grid frameworks.[6] They show that as a technique knitting was well established and, worked perhaps on needles of Toledo steel, could be very fine.

By the middle of the fifteenth century knitting of a coarser kind was produced in England and France. The chief product was caps made of wool, shrunk and matted by fulling after knitting. It has been assumed that the resulting fabric, thick and rather inelastic, would have been unsuitable for stockings and that, consequently, knitted stockings were not worn until much later. However, before fulling the fabric would have been elastic and it is possible that coarse knitted stockings were worn before the beginning of the sixteenth century but at a social level beneath the notice of contemporary historians. Coarse stockings would not have been considered preferable to hose of fine woven material, and cloth of various qualities continued to be worn by all classes well into the seventeenth century, and indeed by some peasant communities into the present century.[7] Woven hose could be cut either along the grain of the fabric or diagonally across it (on the bias), the latter being more elastic, and seamed up the back of the leg. Surviving fragments of Tudor hose in the Museum of London show both the use of a twilled fabric with a diagonal rib which is more elastic than a plain weave, and tubular stockings of coarse knitting with ribbing at the heels. These, however, could date from the later Tudor period, the reign of Elizabeth I, rather than from the reign of Henry VIII. References to knit hose in the first half of the sixteenth century are not plentiful and can be confusing when hose for men could also mean breeches as well as stockings. The mid sixteenth-century knitted breeches[8] in the museum at Dresden are probably exceptional, however, and 'knit hose' in most cases probably does mean knitted stockings.

Hand knitting in England

From near contemporary accounts Henry VIII and his son Edward VI wore principally hose cut from cloth or silk, with only the occasional pair of knitted silk stockings imported at considerable expense from Spain. Sir Thomas Gresham supplied Edward VI with a pair of 'long Spanish silke stockings'[9] and in 1560 sent three pairs of black silk Spanish hose to Lord Burghley for himself and his wife.[10] Henry VIII is recorded as having 'six pairs of black silk hose knit'.[11] His daughter, Mary I, probably had her own source of Spanish knitted stockings through her marriage to Philip II of Spain in 1554 but she was still being supplied with kersey, or cloth, hose; twenty seven pairs from her hosier, Myles Huggarde, in 1554.[12]

By the middle of the century records of knit hose are more plentiful. Francis Willoughby, heir to the Wollaton estates in Nottinghamshire and Thomasine Petre, of Ingatestone, Essex, both

children, had knitted stockings of wool in the 1550s, as well as hose of cloth: Francis's sister Margaret also had a pair of kersey hose in 1550, and Thomasine, hose made of frieze in 1556/7.[13] In 1552 an act for 'limitinge the tymes for levieing and sellying of wolles' mentions 'knitte hose' as well as 'knitte' gloves, sleeves and petticoats.[14] By this time knitted woollen stockings were presumably fairly common but probably rather coarse. Twenty years later, the so-called 'Cappers' Act' of 1571, which decreed that people over the age of six should wear a knitted woollen cap on Sundays and Holy Days, can be seen as an attempt to check the swing away from the knitting of caps towards the knitting of stockings.[15]

Certainly by 1560 there was some fine English knitting. Elizabeth I's first pair of silk stockings, given to her by Mistress Alice Montagu in that year, were English, not Spanish.[16] According to Edward Howes, in his 1614 additions to Stow's *The Annales or Generall Chronicle of England*, the queen liked them so much that she declared 'henceforth I will wear no more cloth stockings'. 'And', continues Howes, 'from that time unto her death, the queene never wore any more cloath hose, but only silke stockings.' In fact it was not so sudden. Elizabeth's Wardrobe Accounts show she was being supplied with about twenty pairs of cloth hose a year until 1577 when she changed to knitted worsted stockings, from Norwich, also supplied by Alice Montagu.[17]

Mary I's worsted stockings, which were probably knitted, had been made on the island of Guernsey. In 1556 Sir Leonard Chamberlain, governor of the island, had given her four pairs.[18] William Rider is credited with being the first to make knitted worsted stockings in England in 1564, by copying a pair he had seen in an Italian merchant's London house.[19] It has been suggested that their novelty lay in their being stockings when only short hose or socks had been knitted before. But the novelty probably lay more in their fineness, being of worsted rather than coarse wool.

Worsted stocking knitting spread. Elizabeth I already possessed Norwich-made worsted stockings when she saw them being knitted on her Progress in August 1578.[20] By 1583, when Philip Stubbs wrote *The Anatomie of Abuses in England*, fine worsted stockings were comparable in price with silk, and even allowing for exaggeration, up to a quarter of a year's wages could be spent on them. Mary, Queen of Scots went to the scaffold in 1587 wearing a pair of blue worsted stockings clocked and edged at the tops with silver, over a pair of white jersey hose, held up with green silk garters.[21] As it was February, wool rather than silk was presumably chosen for warmth, and the finer jersey ones were worn next to the skin. Elizabeth I had 'garnsey knitt Hose wrought at the clockes with silk' and, contradicting her reputation for extravagance, had new feet knitted for four pairs of white worsted hose clocked with gold, silver and silk in 1597.[22]

In the last quarter of the sixteenth century hand knitting was booming. Lee presumably intended to capitalise on this, but, ingenious though his invention was, it could not knit quick enough nor fine enough to command the high fashion market. Traditionally Elizabeth expressed disappointment over the frame's coarse products and asked Lee to adapt his machine to knit silk. She herself wore silk stockings as did her court.

Queen Elizabeth I's silk stockings

A few of the many portraits of Elizabeth I show her shoes but never more than an unrevealing glimpse of stocking. Women's stockings, though hardly ever seen under the long, full skirts, could be very elaborate. In 1562 Eleanora of Toledo, wife of Cosimo I de Medici, Grand Duke of Tuscany, was buried in Florence wearing crimson silk stockings with turnover tops patterned with lattice, and legs with vertical stripes of double moss stitch and double garter stitch. They were made probably in Italy or Spain.[23] Elizabeth I was presented in the same year with 'two pair of silk hose knytt' as a New Year gift by Robert Robotham, Yeoman of the Wardrobe of Robes.[24] Until 1565 her knitted stockings seem to have been mainly of black silk, but by 1588 they were considerably more colourful and elaborate.

Roger Montagu supplied her with five pairs of knitted stockings, carnation pink and other colours 'wrought at the clockes with venice gold and silver' (at £3 6s 8d the pair) and a pair of knitted silk hose 'thinside wrought with carnacion ingraine sleeve silke like unto plush', as well as plain knitted silk stockings. He also redyed four pairs of embroidered silk stockings and refurbished one pair of silk and two pairs of garnsey stockings.

In 1597 Robert Morland supplied the Queen with seven new pairs of silk stockings of different colours 'the clockes richle wrought with gold silver and silke'. Queen Elizabeth also wore linen hose, cut from woven material, presumably as understockings to preserve the silk from perspiration and wear. The only pair of stockings which reputedly belonged to the Queen are preserved at Hatfield House, Hertfordshire. They are, however, knitted in openwork with a pattern of lozenges, quite unlike the solid knitting of the few pairs of stockings, mostly men's, that survive from the late sixteenth and early seventeenth centuries.

Men's stockings

Men's stockings were very visible throughout the sixteenth century. At first they had been either tights covering the leg from foot to waist, or breeches and stockings sewn together and called 'hose'. By the second half of the century they were more usually separate, the breeches being called 'upper stocks' and the stockings 'nether stocks'. The upper stocks could be in various styles, loose and baggy to below the knee, tight or padded out at the hips, with or without tight extensions called 'canions' to above the knee, 'paned', that is cut in strips, or cut from large pieces of material. Nether stocks were cut from cloth but, in the second half of the century, were more often knitted so as to fit closely to the leg.[25] Although most portraits show plain stockings with short clocks that barely cover the ankles, there are a few portraits which depict more elaborate stockings. Cornelius Ketel's portrait of Sir Christopher Hatton, painted in 1582,[26] shows him in white stockings with diagonal bands of patterning presumably in plain and purl knitting, making an inverted V below the knee. The leg and foot appear to be plain but the top of the foot has a tongue onto the leg similar to that of a nineteenth-century riding boot. The tops of the stockings cover the knees and the bottom edge of the gold and black canions. In 1583 Philip Stubbs unleashed a diatribe on expensive, patterned stockings in his *Anatomie of Abuses*: 'Then they have nether stockes to these gay hosen, not of cloth (though never so fine) for that is thought too base, but of jarnsey, worsted, crewell, silke, thread and such like, or else, at the least, of the finest yarn that can be got; and so curiously knit with open seame down the leg, with quirkes and clocks about the ankles, and sometime (haplie) inter-laced about the ancles with gold or silver thread as is wonderful to behold. And to such impudent insolency and shameful outrage it is now growne, that everyone almost, though otherwise very poor, having scarce forty shillings wages by the year, will not stick to have two or three pair of these silk nether stocks, or else of the finest yarn that may be got, though the price of them be a royal, or twenty shillings, or more, as commonly it is; for how can they be lesse, when as the very knitting of them is worth a noble or a royal, and some much more? The time hath been when one might have clothed all his body well, from top to toe, for lesse than a pair of these nether stocks will cost.'[27]

Not surprisingly, few stockings survive from this period. The earliest pair to which a date can be attached is the yellow silk stockings in which Johann III of Sweden was buried in 1594.[28] They have kite-shaped soles and the wales of the clocks run parallel to the sole, rather than to the leg, otherwise they are plain. Stockings buried with Duke Barnim XII of Stettin, Pomerania, in 1603 are similar, except that the angle of the sole at the toe is rounded rather than pointed.[29] A third, brown, stocking from another burial has holes in the hem to tie it above the knee. Similar stockings were worn by Tycho de Brahe, buried in Prague in 1601 and Adam Parniewski, buried in Warsaw in 1614. These latter two might be Spanish, the others might

come from England, Spain or the Low Countries. All of them have suffered to some extent from being buried. A pair of stockings in the collection of the Earl of Rosse at Birr Castle in Ireland come closer to Philip Stubbs's description. They are in salmon pink and gold and silver thread. The legs have a lattice pattern of scrolls incorporating a motif which could be interpreted as a double headed eagle. A similar motif but in a different framework appears in a green, gold and silver knitted jacket[30] in the Lord Middleton Collection at the Museum of Costume and Textiles, Nottingham. In the same collection is a pair of stockings in greenish-yellow silk.[31] The tops have diagonal banding, and below the elaborately embroidered clocks are other clocks formed by purl stitches in the knitting. A fragmentary stocking found on the effigy of James I (died 1625) in Westminster Abbey in 1907 has a similar purl-stitch clock.[32]

From their size the Middleton stockings may have been a boy's and might have been associated with the visit of James I's queen, Anne of Denmark, to Wollaton Hall, the Nottinghamshire home of the Willoughby family, later Barons Middleton, in 1603. Their decoration is sufficiently similar to Elizabeth I's stockings 'wrought with venice gold and silver' for so early a date, but otherwise would compare with portraits of a decade or so later.

Richard Sackville, 3rd Earl of Dorset, as painted by William Larkin in 1613, or by Isaac Oliver in 1616, and Dudley, 3rd Baron North, as painted by an unknown artist in 1614–15, both wear stockings with elaborately embroidered clocks.[33] In the case of the Earl of Dorset the careful correlation between the stockings and the rest of his clothes was no invention of the artist as Sackville's inventories of his wardrobe in 1617–19 show.[34] The scarlet and blue velvet trunk hose embroidered with suns, moons and stars which appears in the Oliver portrait was listed with 'Item one pair of longe watchet [blue] silke stockings embroidered', and also 'Item one pair of lynnen bootehose with tops laced with eight laces of silk, silver and gold.' The black uncut velvet cloak with 'slips' in black satin and gold, the cloth-of-silver doublet

with black slips, and the black grogram trunk hose, which appear in the Larkin portrait, were worn with either black silk stockings embroidered in gold and silver, or white silk stockings embroidered in gold, silver and black. A pair of gold and silver lace-edged black taffeta garters and splendid shoe roses completed the suit. Other outfits had complementary stockings in green, crimson, purple, murrey, tawney, yellow or pearl coloured silks. Nearly all were embroidered, one with 'hartes of gold', and a pair of boothose in the same set had tops of cloth-of-silver embroidered with 'globes, flames and hartes of gold'.

Boothose, as the name suggests, were worn with boots. They were similar to ordinary stockings but their ankles being covered by the boots, could be plain, and the tops would be flared and usually decorated. Surviving boothose of the seventeenth century are of woven linen. A pair in the Victoria and Albert Museum are cut on the bias in one large piece with additional triangles at the tops, and gores at the ankles.[35] Another pair, worn by Gustavus II Adolphus of Sweden (died 1632), are also of linen and have, at the top, a deep cuff embroidered with cornucopiae, flowers and birds, the edge above a row of flowering plants being scalloped.[36] Also in the Livrustkammeren in Stockholm is the pair of stockings worn by the king at his coronation. The top edge is turned down, faced, and stitched with two rows of eyelet holes to lace them to the breeches. The back seams are decorated with an embroidered lattice over a knitted pattern of triangles. The clocks are heavily embroidered in gold thread and sequins to match the doublet and breeches. Though much more elaborate than Richard Sackville's stockings, as befitted a king, they have nevertheless triangles of purl stitch along the heel-sole seams similar to the pair in the Middleton Collection.

Richard Sackville was notoriously extravagant and some of his clothes were later cut

*3 **Left:** Richard Sackville, 3rd Earl of Dorset (1589–1624), by William Larkin, 1613. His white silk stockings are embroidered in black, gold and silver which accords with his doublet and breeches embroidered with stylised honeysuckle. Both the garters and the shoe roses are trimmed with gold and silver lace*

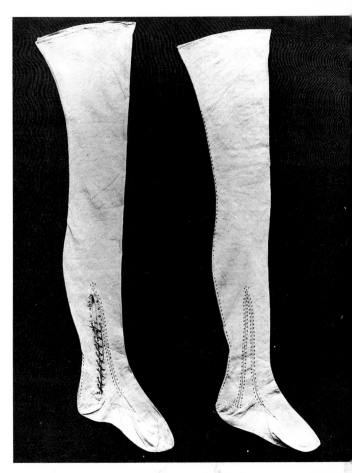

4 Fawn linen stockings, mid seventeenth century; cut on the bias and decorated with detached chain stitch in green; the sole is cut on the straight in white linen and gathered at the heel and toe; the lacing at the gore is presumably to achieve a close fit; from their relative plainness they might have been under-stockings. Length 35 inches, foot length 10 inches

up and used to cover furniture at Knole, the Sackvilles' great house in Kent. But he was not alone. Fynes Moryson commented that whereas in France gentlemen wore stockings of silk 'or of some light stuffe', and only merchants wore woollen or worsted, the English were 'more sumptuous than the Persians.'[37] Their garters and shoe roses were of silk trimmed with gold or silver lace, and their stockings were of silk 'wrought in the seams with silk or gold'. James I, who, during the reign of his predecessor, Elizabeth I, had had to borrow a pair of silk stockings from the Earl of Mar to receive her ambassador, encouraged the extravagant tastes at his court. He tried to start an English silk industry by importing silkworms and planting mulberry trees to feed them.

His son, Charles I, ordered stockings and socks in quantity.[38] In 1633–4 he received from his hosier, Thomas Robinson, sixty pairs of fine silk upper hose, seven pairs of silk under hose, three pairs of thread (linen) hose, fifty-six pairs of fine worsted hose, and sixty-nine pairs of white under hose. The upper and under hose by this period would probably have meant the upper and under stockings of two pairs worn together rather than upper and nether stocks. Not only were they worn for warmth, but also for aesthetic reasons, as the colour would be denser and any hairiness of the legs would be hidden. Even into this century suits with breeches for wear at royal courts were supplied with two pairs of stockings, a silk upper pair and a cotton under pair.

Charles I was also supplied with scarlet silk stockings. These, one may assume, were very expensive as only four pairs were received between 1633 and 1635. Three dozen and eight pairs of boothose with welted tops were supplied by Oliver Seywell in 1633–4, together with four pairs 'scalloped and laced'; whether this meant trimmed with bobbin lace, or supplied with holes and cord for lacing is not stated. Three dozen more pairs were supplied in 1634–5 and a further two dozen 'with welted Topps' in 1635. Interestingly the king was also supplied with stockings for games wear: thirty-five pairs of fine tennis hose, five pairs of tennis silk garters, four dozen pairs of tennis socks, all by Thomas Robinson, and from William Davis sixty-four pairs of 'foote socks' specifically 'for the Tennis and Ballone' in 1633–4, with a further twenty-seven pairs in 1635. Tennis was Royal Tennis played inside an enclosed court. Ballone, according to *Bailey's Dictionary* of 1721 was 'a Football; Also a great Ball with which Noblemen and Princes used to play'. In the same dictionary 'socks' are defined as 'a sort of clothing for the feet' (stockings are not mentioned), and in *Dyche's and Pardon's Dictionary* of 1758 socks are 'something to put at the bottom of the feet,

to keep them warm and dry', in other words 'insoles' and this may be the difference between 'socks' and 'footsocks' supplied to Charles I in the same year. Socks were probably similar to early nineteenth-century half-hose, and foot-socks either insoles or a foot covering.[39] Socks were at least as old as stockings. Henry VIII had a pair of boothose of black cloth and two pairs of 'socks of the same cloth'.[40]

The development of the stocking frame

Even in the middle of the seventeenth century the majority of socks and stockings would have been hand knitted. The use of the stocking frame was, however, growing. On William Lee's death in France, his brother, James, and most of the men he had taken with him, returned to England and set up their frames in London. In the 1620s James, in partnership with William Lee's former apprentice, Aston, who had remained in Nottinghamshire, made new frames incorporating Aston's invention of fixed sinkers between two movable jack sinkers.[41] These made it possible to double the gauge of the machine from William Lee's 12 gauge to 24 gauge and make finer knitting. Probably they also enabled the frame to be worked by one person rather than the two which were needed to work Lee's original frame.

By 1641 there were two master hosiers in Nottingham and an unspecified number of frames. Most frames were, however, in London, close to the king and his court, the centre of fashion. By the time of the Commonwealth the numbers engaged in the craft had grown sufficiently for them to petition Oliver Cromwell for a charter of incorporation, particularly as there was danger of competition from Venice and Amsterdam. In 1656 while their petition was still being considered, Jean Hindret, an industrial spy, smuggled his drawings of the frame out of England into France. They were

5 **Right:** *Henry Rich, 1st Earl of Holland (1590–1649), studio of Daniel Mytens, 1632–3. The turned down tops of his linen boothose are trimmed with densely patterned lace in scallops which echo the scallops on the turndown cuffs of the boot*

Henry Rich: Earl of
Holland.

published a century later by Diderot in his encyclopaedia and provide the only indication of what a seventeenth-century stocking frame looked like.[42] Hindret was able to build several frames from his drawings and to give a start to the French hosiery trade. Considerable skill was still needed to work these frames.

Men's stockings in the mid seventeenth century

The English Civil War probably had little effect on the stocking trade. There might have been an increased demand for boothose and socks by those in the opposing armies and more wearing of wool and less of silk as being more practical. Certainly, judging by the portraits of Charles I's reign, boots were preferred to shoes. The tops of the boothose fell over the tops of the boots and could be bought separately. During 1646–7 James Masters, for instance, purchased a pair of black tops with gold and silver fringe for 3s 6d, red serge tops for 6s and scarlet serge tops for 4s, white riding tops for 5s, and two yards of lace for boothose tops for 11s. He also bought two pairs of 'ancle worsted socks' for 3s 2d, a pair of green silk stockings for 19s in 1647, and a pair of half silk stockings for 9s 6d in 1646.[43] These are likely to have been stockings with wool or linen bottoms and silk tops, and would have been worn as under stockings showing the silk between the top of the boot and boothose and the bottom of the breeches. In the Stapleton Archives there is an entry in 1656 'Paid for a paire of thred bottoms for my topps 1/-'; the tops, of silk, cost 7s 6d.[44] An 'English Anticke' was described in 1646 as wearing 'boot-hose tops, tied about the middle of the calf, as long as a pair of shirt sleeves, double at the ends like a ruff band; the tops of his boots very large, fringed with lace, and turned down as low as his spures, which jingled like the bells of a morrice dancer as he walked'.[45] These large boothose tops were known as 'canons'. In May 1660 Samuel Pepys wroted in his diary: 'Up and made myself as fine as I could with linning [linen] stockings on and wide canons'. Elsewhere he writes of 'knit canons'.[46] The linen stockings might have been cut from woven fabric, but in March 1667 he caught cold through staying bare legged while looking out fresh socks and thread stockings in snowy weather, and these were probably knitted. In the 1640s and 1650s a few portraits of men in shoes show the boothose or upper stocking gartered half way up the leg, the turned-down top flapping untidily.[47]

Men's fashions in the 1650s and early 1660s were extravagant. Short doublets and wide petticoat-breeches were trimmed with yards of ribbon; expensive lace was used to trim shirts and canons. On the 8 October 1666 Charles II declared that he would set a new fashion for clothes 'to teach the nobility thrift', and a week later put on a new suit, a black cloth waistcoat, pinked, with white silk showing under it, a coat and breeches. Pepys describes the King's legs as being 'ruffled with black riband like a pigeon's leg'.[48] The new fashion meant the eventual end of boothose as fashionable wear and attention concentrated on the stocking above the high-heeled shoe.

Women's stockings

Women's stockings throughout the seventeenth century were completely hidden by their skirts. Only occasionally are there references in inventories and accounts, which suggest that they were by no means dull. In 1650 a pair of scarlet silk stockings and a pair of Turkey garters were bought for a lady of the Verney family.[49] In the 1670s even the daughters of George Fox, the Quaker, had red, white, sea-green or sky-coloured worsted stockings.[50] Women's stockings generally are likely to have been plain or with purl-stitch decoration at the ankles. One of three pairs of red stockings left by Charles X Gustavus of Sweden on his death in 1660 are decorated in this way and women's stockings were probably similar.[51]

Equally scanty is the evidence for what is worn by the common people. Ellin, a servant of Ieu'n ap Rees ap David, in Wales, received between 1580 and 1610 both hose of cloth and fine kersey, and woollen hose knitted by her sister Elinor or by the daughter of Thomas ap

John Griffiths, sometimes of yarn of Ellin's own spinning. The woollen hose cost 9d, the knitted hose was a penny dearer, knitting by itself cost 4d, but the fine kersey hose were more expensive still at 14d.[52] In July 1667 Samuel Pepys noted that a shepherd he talked to on Epsom Downs wore shoes shod round with iron and 'woolen knit stockings of two colours mixed'. In general, knitted stockings of wool were likely to be rather coarse, as they would have been made from short staple, the short fibres from the fleece, carded with wooden combs with iron spikes, and spun by hand, or on the great, or treadleless, wheel. The longer fibres were, by contrast, combed and spun using the small Guernsey or Jersey wheel into worsted, a thinner, stronger yarn. Norfolk was the great centre in England for worsted weaving and knitting.

6   Hand knitted green silk stocking, mid seventeenth century; silver thread forms chevrons below the welt, zigzags either side of the centre back, the outline of the clock, and the palmette. Length $19\frac{1}{2}$ inches, foot length $8\frac{1}{4}$ inches, 20 stitches per inch down the leg, 12 stitches per inch at the sole and toe

2
1670–1750

Hand knitted stockings in England and Scotland

The last quarter of the seventeenth century saw not only the hand knitting industry firmly established but also the beginnings of serious competition from the stocking frame.

Since the introduction of knitting into England, the English had found that it met some sort of national need, for they had speedily become very adept at it. Fynes Moryson commented in 1617 that English stockings were superior to both Italian and Spanish ones.[1] The anonymous French writer of *Les Lois de la Galanterie* (1644) recommended that 'those who wear silk stockings should always have English ones'.[2] Areas of the country where knitting was prevalent were noted by Celia Fiennes, who rode through England in the 1690s and Daniel Defoe, who published his *Tour* between 1722 and 1726, basing it partly on his travels in the 1680s, perhaps in connection with his work as hose-factor or wholesaler.

These areas were chiefly the areas of wool production. Aulnage records point to the country around Norwich in Norfolk, and around Richmond and Doncaster in Yorkshire, as being the prime centres. But Devon and Cornwall were knitting enough to export to Flushing, Amsterdam and Dieppe, and Nottinghamshire and Leicestershire were already recognised as knitting areas. By the early eighteenth century knitting was established in Cheshire, Westmorland, Dentdale and Garsdale, and by the end of the century in Somerset and Essex. Welsh stockings were sold in Surrey in the 1670s.[3]

Celia Fiennes commented on the knitting of wool in Norwich and Wymondham, and the area around Attleborough, all in Norfolk, and of cotton in Gloucester.[4] Defoe noted that stockings were made at Tewkesbury, Gloucestershire, Pershore and Evesham, Worcestershire, on the Isle of Purbeck, Dorset, and that Stourbridge, Dorset, was 'once famous for making the finest, best and highest prized knit stockings in England.'[5] Richmond, in Yorkshire, held a market for woollen and yarn stockings, of which Defoe said: 'they make very coarse and ordinary, and they are sold accordingly; for the smallest sized stockings for children are here sold for eighteen pence per dozen, or three halfpence a pair, sometimes less'.[6] Richmond was also the marketing centre for stockings made in Westmorland, Kendal and Kirkby Stephen. The making of yarn stockings extended as far as Barnard Castle, County Durham. Defoe regarded Nottingham and Leicester more as centres of framework knitting and saw their products for sale at the Sturbridge Fair in Cambridgeshire. Aberdeen, like Norfolk, made very fine worsted stockings, some selling for between fourteen and twenty shillings a pair. Many were exported to Norway, Holland, Portugal, Spain and Germany.[7]

A pair of boothose in the Victoria and Albert Museum is knitted in cream wool in the round but with imitation back seams in purl stitch, a correlation point for the knitter in increasing and decreasing.[8] The 'seams' are embellished with an embroidered herringbone in blue wool. The clocks are relatively short with three or four lines of blue along the heel and foot to two lozenges and scrolls. Similar lozenges appear on the stockings of a male corpse buried at Tawnamore, County Sligo, in the late seventeenth century, and on the under stockings on the funeral effigies of James I and the Duchess of Richmond and Lennox in Westminster Abbey.[9] At the knee the boothose have a band of vertical ribbing and then flare out quite considerably to a circumference of 37½ inches. Bands of purl lozenges with a band of four blue lines decorate the cuff on the outside, so that it was intended to be worn up and not folded down. Randle Holme in the *Academie of Armourie* (1688) mentions: 'Large stirrup hose or stockings, two yards wide at the top, with points through several ilet holes by which they were made fast to the petticoat-breeches by a single row of pointed ribbons hanging at the bottom.'[10] These boothose are not as large, nor have they any visible means of support in the way of eyelet holes. They were either supported by the cuff of the boot, in which case much of the decoration would be hidden, or pinned to the breeches. A pair of breeches in the Isham Collection has a

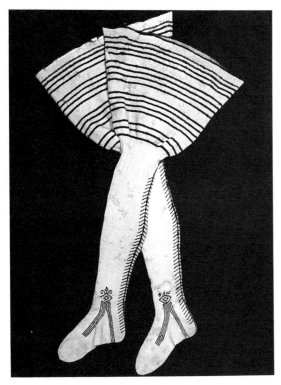

7   *Hand knitted boothose, in cream wool with embroidered decoration in navy blue wool, 1650–80; the hose are knitted in the round with all the decoration on the outside of the cuff; the band of ribbing at the knee would help to keep the cuff up and prevent the garter from slipping. Length 38 inches, foot length 10¼ inches, circumference at top 37½ inches*

caught-up frill at each knee, in what may be a similar style.[11] These boothose, traditionally made at Waddon in Dorset, probably date from between 1650 and 1680. Boothose generally passed out of fashion when shoes replaced boots as fashionable wear in the 1650s and 1660s.

Hand knitting succeeded in many areas because it could be easily fitted in between chores or during slack periods in seasonal jobs such as farming or fishing. In pastoral communities the raw material was to hand, but even elsewhere it could be imported or exchanged. Between 1650 and 1750 it came under competition from the stocking frame. In 1724 Defoe blamed the decay of the hand knitted stocking trade on 'the increase of the knitting-stocking engine or frame, which had destroyed the hand knitting trade for fine stockings through the whole kingdom'.[12] It was the fineness that was the frames' chief advantage. 'Knit stockings are much more preferable in durableness and strength to those made in the loom [frame], but the time employed in knitting stockings of any fineness raises their price too much for common wear.'[13] For coarser stockings, because there was little in the way of extra costs, unlike the rent charged on leased frames, whether working or not, hand knitting was still preferred and continued to be so for much of the eighteenth century.

Improvements to the stocking frame

Careful comparison between Hindret's drawings of 1656 and the engraving of Thomas Sandby's drawings for Deering's *History of Nottingham* (1751) show that the stocking frame was still being developed.[14] By the end of the century British inventive skills had added trucks or wheels to bear the weight of the working parts of the machine as they moved forward and back in knitting, sleys which prevented the jacks from moving sideways and, by 1711, caster backs, hanging bits and front stops. All these adaptations which enabled the frame to work more smoothly and make much more regular loops and rows, gave the English an edge over their rivals, the French. The numbers of frames increased from 650 (400 of which were in

London) in about 1660, to 1500 in London alone in 1695. Between 1670 and 1695, however, 400 frames were exported to France, Italy and Spain despite the new charter granted by Charles II in 1663 which specifically forbade the export of 'any frames used for making silk stockings.'[15] Under William III, fines were instituted and a system of numbering the frames so that a check could be kept on them.[16] Charles II's charter also established a self-perpetuating oligarchy of a master, two wardens and fifteen or more liverymen of the Company of Framework Knitters, all of whom were appointed for life. This, and the fact that it was essentially concerned with stocking making in London, was to bear fruit for both the London and Midland hosiery trades by the middle of the eighteenth century.

Colour in stockings in England, France and Scotland

The fashionable silk stocking trade established itself and grew in London because only there could it react quickly enough to changes in fashion, and, because it was modish to have stockings matching or at least harmonizing with the suit, it made sense to have stockings made near to where the suit was made. Hindret's frames were set up first in Paris for the same reason, with Nîmes becoming the centre for the woollen trade.

The monochrome example set by Charles II for the English court in 1666 was not followed by the French court, least of all by the French king, Louis XIV. On visits to the Academy of Sciences and to the Gobelin factory in 1667 he wore scarlet stockings to match his hat feathers and ribbon knots at neck, cuffs and shoulders. His courtiers wore brown, white, red, blue and grey stockings at his entry into Arras in July of that year.[17] On such a formal occasion these could have been of silk or fine worsted. Guernsey had a lucrative trade in the 1670s supplying the wealthy nobles and bourgeoisie of Paris with worsted stockings. One dealer used no less than thirty three code numbers to identify his stock which included three grades of marbled hose,

8 *Blue silk stocking with 'turn shape' decoration; dated 1700 when shown by J R Allen at the Great Exhibition in 1851. Length 25 inches, foot length 10 inches, 28 stitches per inch, 28 rows per vertical inch*

red striped stockings, and others in white, blue striped white, greyish white, greyish brown, iron-grey, blue and white and black.[18]

In Scotland in the 1680s, the New Mills Woollen Manufactory at Haddington produced white silk stockings, which were then dyed black, and flirted with buff and grass-green ready-dyed silk before abandoning silk in favour of red, gold, green, buff, blue and black worsted.[19] But the worsted was unevenly spun and the Manufactory reverted to marbled silk before largely abandoning stocking production in 1688. The marbled silk was either of two different colours twisted together or of silk printed or space dyed with random bands of colour.

The New Mills Woollen Manufactory was set

up under the patronage of the Duke of York by Robert Blackwood, Master of the Edinburgh Merchants Company, and Sir James Stanfield, MP for Haddington in 1682. Its aim was to produce sufficient wool and silk textiles of high quality for the home market. This speculative venture was not a success but by the early years of the eighteenth century there were framework knitters in Edinburgh producing silk, silk and worsted, and worsted stockings. By 1739 even thread and cotton hose were being made.

Stocking knitting industries in France and Russia

Scotland was not the only country to start knitting manufactories. By an edict of 30 March 1700 hosiery production in France was limited to eighteen centres: Paris, Dourdon, Rouen, Caen, Nantes, Olleron, Aix, Toulouse, Uzes, Romas, Lyons, Metz, Bourges, Poitiers, Orleans, Amiens, Reims and Nîmes.[20] Of these Paris produced fashionable hosiery and Nîmes hosiery of wool, or wool and silk (called *d'etamine*) and later of poor quality silk in vast quantitites for export to Northern Europe, Spain and Spanish colonies in South America. Some of the frames had earlier been worked by Huguenots and following the Revocation of the Edict of Nantes in 1685 and the consequent persecution of Protestants, many Huguenots, with their frames, fled from France to Germany.

Peter I (1672–1725) encouraged Huguenot and German framework knitters to move to Russia, but the first successful factory, of four frames, was set up under a Frenchman in Moscow in 1704. By 1737 it was supplying ten thousand pairs of wool stockings for the army, as well as beaver and silk mixtures and silk by itself.[21]

Three pairs of Peter I's stockings survive. Two are of machine knitted red silk and one has had the embroidered clocks cut out for re-use, an indication of how expensive stockings were. The third pair is also machine knitted in light fawn and grey-blue wool and silk mixture. The first two pairs are considered to be imports, the third possibly the production of the Moscow factory.[22]

Gore clocks

Improvements to the stocking frame had concentrated on making machines which produced a finer, more regular fabric. Until the end of the seventeenth century no attempt was made to make the stocking itself more decorative. As men took to wearing shoes instead of boots, the lower leg, and the stocking covering it, became a focus of interest. In the 1670s, as made on the frame, the stocking was a flat piece of fabric, shaped at the sides for the calf and the ankle, with heel flaps, which had to be joined together under the heel, and, between them, the top of the foot to the toe. The sole was made separately and sewn to the toe, the sides of the foot and the front of the heel flaps. During the same decade it was discovered that the top of the foot could be made narrower and the fronts of the heel flaps longer so that a wedge shape appeared over the ankle. As the point of this wedge extended upwards in the 1680s it was found easier to make it separately as a gore, and seam it in. Usually, to accommodate the ankle bone, the wales of the gore run parallel with the sole and at right angles to the wales of the leg. By the 1690s these gores had reached the lower calf and were often of a contrasting colour to the rest of the stocking. As a further embellishment the stocking round the gore could be embroidered, often in a colour to match the gore. This embroidery was often quite slight, scrolls either side of the gore, and a crown, coronet, or rose above the point. It was probably professional rather than amateur work. Isobel Hunter, for example, was bound apprentice for five years to Barbara Henderson in Edinburgh in 1695, to be taught 'embroidery of all sorts, white seam, lace and stocking-working' as well as 'drawing and draughts' and writing.[23]

The fashion for gore clocks is one of the most decorative developments in the history of the stocking and yet it is barely recorded. The increasing height of the gore can be traced in the fashion plates that were being produced in Paris for circulation throughout Europe. Fortunately some of them, especially those by Jean de Saint-Jean from the 1670s into the 1690s are of high quality, yet, even in these, the embroidery around the clock is only sketched in, not drawn in detail. Many of the portraits of this period are half or three-quarter length and do not show the stockings. Literary references are tantalisingly few. Dangeau's *Journal* mentions silk stockings of various colours with gold clocks worn at the marriage of the Duke of Burgundy and the Princess of Savoy in 1697.[24] These clocks could either have been knitted or embroidered.

In *A Voyage to Marryland* part of *Mundus Muliebris*, or the *Ladies Dressing-Room Unlock'd*, published by John Evelyn in 1690, Mary Evelyn (1665–85) lists:

> 'Four pair of Bas de Soy [silk stockings] shot through
> With silver, diamond Buckles too,
> For Garters, and as rich for Shoo'

as part of the trousseau a prospective husband would have to provide. These stockings are further defined in the second part, *The Fop*

Dictionary, as 'Silk Stokings [sic] with gold, or silver thread wove into the clock.'[25]

Two stockings which would match this description are in the Middleton Collection at the Museum of Costume and Textiles, Nottingham.[26] Both are knitted in a brown and fawn speckled silk with a silver thread. The gore clocks are knitted silver thread over knitted white silk and the decoration is knitted in at the top of the clock; the scrolls are plated. All that is known of them is that they were worn by a member of the Willoughby family, but it is possible that they were worn with a superb court suit, in the same collection, made for the coronation of George I in 1715.

Neither of the two historians of the early hosiery trade, Henson nor Felkin, give a firm date for the introduction of gore clocks nor turn shapes, the other form of decoration seemingly popular at this period. 'Turn shapes' imitate on the frame the purl-stitch decoration of hand knitting. Individual loops are caught by the needle held in the hand, and are then relooped by two, three or more pressings so that the end result is an indented pattern. Turn shapes are usually in the form of thin scrolls, hearts and lozenges. The earliest dated example of this type of work, though the dating is not contemporary, is a stocking in the Museum of Costume and Textiles, Nottingham.[27] Labelled as a stocking of 1700 it was exhibited along with nine other labelled stockings, unlabelled half-hose and foot 'sox' at the Great Exhibition in London in 1851, by J R Allen of Allen and Solly, Nottingham.

The 1700 stocking is not the only one of this style. The funeral effigy of the Duchess of Buckingham in Westminster Abbey has stockings of pink silk with turn shape decoration extending up to the lower calf.[28] It is quite elaborate, consisting of two vertical rows of scrolls enclosing a heart between four lozenges

9 **Left:** *Stockings, second quarter of the eighteenth century:* Left, *machine knitted pink silk, green silk gore clock with plated decoration each side and at top. Length 22½ inches, foot length 8¼ inches, 24 stitches per inch. Right, machine knitted green silk, pink silk gore clock, plated decoration. Length 24¼ inches, foot length 9½ inches, 24 stitches per inch*

with an inverted heart between flowers and scrolls above. The stockings also have a welt which replaces the band of ribbing or fancy stitches to be found on hand made stockings as these were laborious and time-consuming to make on the machine. Both the welt and the band had the practical purpose of preventing the stocking slipping below the garter. The stockings are, however, different in the shape of the sole. The sides of the soles on the Duchess's stockings when laid flat, curve outwards in a flare, whereas those of the 1700 stocking are almost straight. Henson ascribes the invention of this shaping to a Charles Villiers, a master stockinger, who was very proud of his shapely legs and gave detailed instructions for the precise narrowing of the stocking leg to his workmen.[29] When these became standard, according to Henson, 'the English silk and cotton stockings became decidedly superior in shape to those of any other country...and in fine silk stockings...has caused them always to be preferred to French, Spanish or Italian'. Catherine Sedley, Duchess of Buckingham, was very proud of her royal blood (albeit illegitimate) and when her son, Edmund Sheffield, 2nd and last Duke of Buckingham, died in 1732 she supervised the making and dressing not only of his funeral effigy, but of her own as well. The stockings, which appear unworn, therefore probably belong to the period from just prior to 1732 up to 1743 when she died. Henson gives no date for Villiers's improvement but mentions it apropos of a framework knitters' petition to Parliament in 1753.

Gore clocks to the mid eighteenth century and beyond

None of the stockings mentioned is obviously for either a man or a woman. Those glimpsed on women in undress in the fashion plates have clocks too, and there was probably little, if any, difference between the stockings of both sexes. Gore clocks, six or seven inches high, continued into the eighteenth century. They echoed the fashionable silhouette which was, for women, accentuated by the frelange headdress, a tower-

10 Left: _machine knitted green silk with 7 inch high pink clock, over-embroidered in white silk satin stitch. Length 19½ inches, foot length 8 inches, 24 stitches per inch_ Right: _machine knitted green silk, 6 inch high white clock, embroidered above with bird and flower in silver. Length 21 inches, foot length 8 inches, 24–28 stitches per inch. Both stockings 1720–40; neither has a welt but part of the banding at the top was probably once folded and sewn down. Clause 2 of the Tewkesbury Act (1765) directed 'The act not to prevent manufacturers using remnants in welts and tops of stockings, only not to exceed three inches...'_

ing structure of frills on a wire frame, and, in men, by narrow breeches, tight coats, and by rolling the stockings over the knees of the breeches. Both sexes wore high heels to their shoes, the men's often red.

There are stockings with gore clocks in several museum collections. Pickford's House Museum in Derby has a pink silk pair with green clocks and decoration around the clocks which is 'plated', that is laid on top of the foundation colour.[30] The Gallery of English Costume, Manchester, has a similar pink pair with green clocks and a pair of green with pink clocks.[31] The Museum of London's green silk stockings have, however, white silk embroidery over the pink clocks.[32]

'Blue Stockings'

Although the gore retained its height into the 1750s it became narrower and the decorative embroidery more attenuated until the gore itself disappeared and only slight embroidery remained. In less fashionable dress the gore continued at least until the end of the century. An advertisement in the *Chester Chronicle*, 1790, offered 'Stockings made of the person's own stuff at the following rates: Women's outsize gore clox 1s 8d; Women's common size gore clox 1s 6d; Women's common size turned clox 1s 4d.'[33] A late eighteenth century coloured print after a painting by Francis Wheatley, of a miller and his inamorata, shows her in blue stockings with red clocks, and him in blue stockings, badly gartered. As an Italian or Austrian peasant girl at a masquerade in 1814, Harriette Wilson wore blue silk stockings with small red clocks. But she wore plain blue stockings, thick shoes, blue check apron, 'clothcap, bright cherry-coloured ribbons' when she went to Oxford disguised as a country girl for a clandestine meeting with the Marquis of Worcester in about 1810.[34]

Blue was a very popular colour for working class clothing. Mary Morgan, a poor Irish woman, wore a brown frieze jacket, scarlet frieze petticoat, green serge apron and blue worsted stockings in the mid eighteenth century.[35] The dye was indigo, probably bulked out with woad, and was cheap. One explanation of the term 'Blue Stocking' applied to members of the Society of Literati which met at Mrs Montagu's house in the mid eighteenth century is that they were so uncaring about their dress that they would wear even working class blue stockings. Other accounts trace the term back via a French salon in the seventeenth century to the Society de la Calza (stocking) in Venice in the fifteenth and sixteenth centuries.[36] The English nickname, on the contrary, is said to have been inspired by the blue stockings which Benjamin Stillingfleet, one of the founder members, habitually wore. Since so many of the group were women, the term 'blue stocking' became synonymous with intellectual or literary ladies. Along with blue, pink was also worn by the working classes, and made for them in Leicester.[37]

Embroidered stockings

In addition to the gore clock, there are numerous references to gold and silver clocked stockings in contemporary letters and accounts chiefly in the 1720s and 1730s. It is often not stated, however, whether these are gold or silver gore clocks, or embroidered clocks.

The Marquis of Carmarthen had a couple of pairs of black silk stockings with gold or silver clocks in 1728,[38] and a beau of 1727 wore with Mechlin lace, a laced coat and black velvet breeches 'red heels to his shoes and gold clocks to his stockings'.[39] Some of these stockings were probably made in France, Holland or Italy. Pole Cosby bought 'four pair of silver and gold clocked silver stockings' in Holland to wear with crimson Genoa velvet and brocade at Viceregal Courts in Dublin in the 1720s.[40] In Hogarth's paintings gold or silver clocked stockings are associated with foppish, if not Frenchified, clothes. In *The Rake's Progress*, 1733, the rake wears gold clocked red stockings with a gold laced blue coat and tie wig with a huge bag and solitaire when he is arrested (Scene IV) and in prison (Scene VII). Elsewhere his stockings are white or pale blue.[41] In *The Four Times of Day*, 1736, 'Noon' depicts a French couple leaving the French church in Hog Lane, Soho. The man is wearing a laced orange coat and waistcoat, black breeches and gold clocked red stockings.[42] The portrait of Prince Charles Edward Stuart, 'The Young Pretender', in which he wears gold clocked white

11 **Right:** *Detail from 'The Rake at the Rose Tavern', Scene III of 'The Rake's Progress' by William Hogarth, 1733. A prostitute is undressing. Her stockings are blue with scarlet zigzags and a coronet above the scarlet gore clock. The garters are also scarlet*

stockings was painted in Rome in 1738.[43] These are embroidered around a gore clock, but there are other stockings in which the metal thread embroidery either covers the gore or replaces it. Examples of this style are in both the Victoria and Albert Museum and the Museum of London.[44] A pair of brown silk stockings with elaborately embroidered silver clocks which complement a silver embroidered brown wool coat is in the Museum of Costume at Bath. The coat and stockings were worn by Sir Thomas Kirkpatrick of Closeburn, Fife (1704–1771) in about 1720.[45] Continental portraits show a similar style of embroidery in white silk on colours or white.[46] Examples of this style of stocking in the Museum of London might owe something to the Huguenot community of silk weavers in Spitalfields. The embroidery varies from elaborate professional work to rather crude flowers in coarse satin stitch. These might be later and perhaps worn further down the social scale, or may be of amateur workmanship.

Embroidered stockings fit into the context of embroidered costume, particularly fashionable from the 1720s to the 1740s. The magnificent mantuas in the Victoria and Albert Museum, and the aprons, shoes and stomachers in other collections testify to the generality of the fashion. Contemporary letters bear this out. Mrs Delany, herself a fine embroideress, frequently comments on the embroidery she sees and describes some in detail: Lady Huntingdon's black velvet petticoat, for example, worked with 'a large stone vase filled with ramping flowers' in 1738–9.[47]

Ribbed stockings and the tuck presser

Yet another style of stocking was ribbed. Some ribbing is mentioned in the late seventeenth century but it may have been largely unfashionable. Its existence may be deduced from the invention of the tuck presser, a thin bar of iron with grooves on the underside and teeth which would admit some loops and hold others behind. A 'tuck' is 'the technical term for two or three loops accumulated on the same needle'.[48] By giving the bar a slight sideways shift, ribs of these accumulated loops could be made and, by

shifting it even further, a zigzag effect. There is some doubt as to who invented the tuck presser and when. French framework knitters in the early nineteenth century claimed the invention for Louis XIV who was, apparently, as adept at framework knitting as his descendant, Louis XVI was at lock making, but it seems to have come into general use twenty years or so after the former's death.[49] Henson gives no date for its invention and places its introduction into Nottingham by an Irish stockinger between 1735 and 1742.[50] Felkin suggests between 1740 and 1756.[51] In this context the premium awarded to Michael Bone by the Dublin Society on 15 January 1741 might have some relevance. It was for 'making ribbed stockings and twilling them withinside', a description which would fit the use of the tuck presser.[52] This invention does not appear to have been used in London. Already the mechanical initiatives lay with Nottingham and the workforce was gradually leaving London for the Midlands where food and fuel were cheaper and less control was exercised by the Framework Knitters Company. In the country a master could take as many apprentices, both male and female, as he had frames for, whereas in London he was restricted to three men.

Changes in fashion: from colour to white

Until the 1730s, as the colour of the stockings complemented the colour of the suit or dress, there had been an advantage in having stockings made in London, close to where the silks were woven in Spitalfields, but during the 1730s there was a shift in fashion from coloured stockings with full or formal dress to white. *Read's Weekly Journal* commented in 1736 'white stockings were universally worn by the gentlemen as well as the ladies' at a royal wedding.[53] In the same year *The Leeds Mercury* reported that at a royal ball 'there were scarce any other coloured stockings worn than plain white' and these chiefly by ladies to complement white shoes, braided with gold or silver.[54] Silk in general was not washed after the manufacturing process, but boarded, that is stretched over a leg-shaped board, and flattened under a weight. White silk

12 **Left:** *Brown silk stocking (one of a pair) with silver thread and purl embroidery of stylised fruits; originally worn by Sir Thomas Kirkpatrick of Closeburn, Fife (1704–1771) with a brown wool coat, similarly embroidered in silver, and breeches: c 1720. Length 34 inches, foot length 10 inches*

'Make your petticoats short, that a hoop eight yards wide
May decently show how your garters are tied.' (1753)[56]

Garters were now of thin strips of braid or 'ferreting'. Some were woven with mottoes, political or amorous. A pair of 1717 in the Gallery of English Costume are woven with 'My heart is fixt, I cannot range' and 'I like my choice too well to change.'[57] Others of *c*1659 have 'God Bless P.C. [Prince Charles] and down with the Rump' [the 'Rump' Parliament of 1648–59]. Garters with 'No Search' were advertised for sale in Colchester in 1739.[58]

Silk and other stockings compared

Silk stockings were expensive. Until the eighteenth century they were often supplied by the tailor with the suit. A member of the Isham family paid, in 1681, 14s for a pair of silk stockings out of a total bill of £4 13s for a dove colour silk coat and breeches and white satin waistcoat.[59] In 1689 William III's tailor, Robert Graham, included stockings in his charge of £2 10s for making a suit but excluded the cloth.[60] Buttons and trimmings could cost over three times the cost of the making. George Thomson (1717–81?), a gentleman of average means who was studying the law in the late 1730s and early 1740s paid £1 2s for a pair of silk stockings in February 1738/9. Usually he paid 14s per pair, and 5s a pair for both worsted and thread stockings. Cotton stockings cost the same or were a shilling dearer. The cheapest stockings he bought cost 2s 6d a pair in December 1739. A suit, probably without a waistcoat, cost £8 4s in 1741.[61]

Tobias Smollett's *Roderick Random* (1748, but written in about 1739), and Samuel Richard-

was the most difficult to work as every spot or blemish showed. But white had its merits: 'A Lady's leg is a dangerous sight in whatever colour it appears, but when it is enclosed in white it makes an irresistible attack upon us.'[55] The hooped petticoat, introduced in 1709, and assuming various shapes . . . domed, square, fan-shaped, oblong . . . throughout much of the eighteenth century, made a glimpse of stocking even more likely as it swung or was caught by the breeze.

13 *Sir Wolstan Dixie by Henry Pickering, 1746.*
White silk stockings are worn with crimson velvet coat
and breeches, and a gold embroidered white satin
waistcoat.The clocks are narrow gores, slightly
embroidered at the edge and with a trefoil at the top.
Despite the landscape background this is full, or formal,
dress

son's *Pamela* (1740) show perhaps more clearly than account books the social gradations of the fibre of stockings. Setting out for London Roderick is supplied with money to buy a suit of clothes, a dozen shirts and 'two pair of worsted stockings, as many thread' as well as a case of surgical instruments and two books. Later a former shipmate gives him 'half a dozen fine shirts, and as many linen waistcoats and caps, with twelve pair of new thread stockings' and he begins 'to look upon myself as a gentleman of some consequence'. In Paris he has five fashionable coats of cut velvet or gold and silver trimmed, two frocks (coats with collars), seven waistcoats, eight pairs of breeches, 'twelve pair of white silk stockings, as many of black silk, and the same number of fine cotton', perhaps as under stockings. By contrast, his uncle, the lieutenant of a man-of-war, wears grey worsted stockings.[62] Pamela, a superior maid servant, is given on her mistress's death 'four pair of fine white cotton stockings and three pair of fine silk ones'. When she decides to return to her clergyman father's home, she buys 'two pairs of ordinary blue worsted hose, that make a smartish appearance with white clocks, I'll assure you!.' Dressed as a lady she wears 'fine white cotton stockings' with silk shoes and a green silk gown and petticoat.[63]

Though Pamela bought some stockings from a pedlar, as the non-fictional Parson Woodforde was to do later in the century, stockings could also be bought from haberdashers, hosiers, or hosiers in combination with other trades. Worsted, thread and silk stockings were supplied to the 4th Duke of Bedford and his family by William Wilmot, hosier, at the sign of the Black Lion in Norfolk Street, Strand, or by Nisbett and Masters, hosiers and hatters, at the Queen's Head in Queen Street, Cheapside in the 1740s and 1750s.[64] As the manufacturing of stockings moved out of London, more hosiers took to retaining rooms in London inns. By the 1760s many of these rooms were no more than stockrooms, and one inn, The Cross Keys in Wood Street, held the stocks of no less than fourteen provincial hosiers.[65] The framework knitting trade was on the verge of great expansion.

3

1750–1800

During the second half of the eighteenth century the English middle class grew steadily more prosperous through industrial enterprise and trade inside and outside an expanding empire which by 1765 included India, North America and the West Indies. Its demands for more and finer stockings inspired technical innovation and finally tipped the balance against the hand knitter. By 1750 framework knitting, even of silk, had broken away from the domination of London. Most framework knitters were now concentrated in the East Midlands, in towns, or in villages where they combined knitting with small scale farming. Outside the range of the Framework Knitters Company they took as many apprentices as they pleased, cheap labour for themselves but increasing the number of semi-skilled workmen. As frames, particularly with new and patented improvements, were expensive, most stockingers rented them from hosiers. Rent was paid on frames whether working or not and many households had two. They were a safe investment for those with a little spare capital but the framework knitter was put in a vulnerable position when times were hard or work short. During this half century, too, experiments on the stocking frame gave birth to machine-made lace; many skilled hands were seduced to its higher profits. The former independent-minded framework knitter, working his own frame three days a week, gardening or making music in his leisure time was ultimately transformed into a drudge incessantly working to provide his family with the bare necessities. The beginnings of this change could be seen in the 1780s.[1]

Of more immediate moment in 1750, however, was a competition to decide whether France or England made the better stockings. Joseph Stocks of England operated a 38 gauge frame, the finest then in existence, but still the French stockings were judged superior in fineness, workmanship and texture. English expertise turned from the finer gauge machine to the fabric and fibre of the stocking itself, and initially to making ribbed stockings by machine.[2]

Derby Ribs

As knitted by hand, the ribbed stocking has stripes of plain knitting showing alternately the right side and the wrong side on the face. The ribs can vary in the number of wales on the front and back, which can be even, eg 2:2, or uneven, eg 3:2, and narrow or wide. They seem to have been popular in the 1740s and early 1750s. Commodore Keppel wears wide ribbed stockings in his portrait of 1752 by Reynolds.[3] They are probably hand knitted. A pair of speckled silk stockings in the Victoria and Albert Museum are hand knitted with ribs three quarters of an inch wide and probably date from the first half of the eighteenth century though they could be later.[4]

Apart from the tuck rib, which seems to have been a rib in appearance only, the first attempts to make a ribbed stocking on the frame were by hand, by dropping the stitches and laboriously relooping each wale. This was first done by a workman named Wright at Ilkeston, Derbyshire, in 1730, and he was paid half-a-guinea (10s 6d) for them. Twenty years later one Bowman, at Dale Abbey, near Ilkeston, succeeded in making ribs on the same principle but relooping several wales at a time by needles fixed in a wooden block.[5] However, it was Jedediah Strutt, son of a landowner near Alfreton, Derbyshire, who achieved the perfect rib. To the front of the

frame he added an apparatus with needles set almost vertically to go between the frame's horizontal needles. The number of needles and the intervals between them dictated the size of the rib. Strutt patented his machine in 1758 (No.722) and, in 1759 (No.734), in partnership with his father-in-law, and later with Samuel Need of Nottingham, set up business in Derby.[6] Consequently his ribbed stockings were known as 'Derby Ribs'. Those made in worsted or cotton were very popular, 'but those made of silk, from some inexplicable cause, though they are most beautiful and excellent sound article, and very elastic have never been much in request'.[7] By the 1830s cotton ribbed hose, nearly all of which were British made, went out of fashion and out of production, though worsted Derby Rib stockings continued to be made. All ribbed hose had toes and soles made on the plain frame.[8] Sadly no museum appears to have a pair of eighteenth-century Derby Rib stockings.

Imitation ribs

Ribs not only fit more closely, hence their continuing popularity for men's socks, but also make the leg look slimmer. The disadvantage of both hand and machine ribs is that the stocking's surface is uneven. Various attempts were made to make hose that appeared to be ribbed but were in fact flat. William Horton took out two patents, in 1771 (No.991, with Richard Marsh) and in 1776 (No.1120) for knotted hosiery.[9] He used points, one to each needle, which, by a sideways movement lifted the loop off one needle and moved it to the next. By moving the loops in one direction for several rows and then reversing the action a ribbed effect was made by the diagonal threads catching the light in different ways. The ribs so produced were horizontal, consequently all stockings made in this

way are knitted across the frame, cut to shape and seamed up the back with the raw edges inside.

Horton doubled the size of the frame, from the standard 15 inches to 30, and even constructed two frames 54 inches wide which his workmen in Godalming, Surrey, nicknamed 'Gog' and 'Magog' after the legendary British giants. Only one machine was worked the full width, by a man named Whitehorn, to make fleecy great-coats.[10]

15   Silk stocking, mid eighteenth century; white silk twisted with lavender and green silk to give a brown, speckled appearance; the chevron welt is a feature of hand knitted stockings; the ribs are 16:16 and three quarters of an inch wide. Length 28¼ inches, foot length 10 inches, 28 stitches per inch

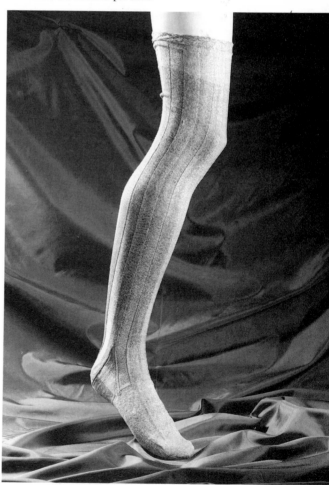

*14   **Left:** Commodore Augustus Keppel (1725–86), engraving (1759) by Edward Fisher, after the portrait by Sir Joshua Reynolds 1752. He is dressed in a blue coat with grey facings, waistcoat and breeches, trimmed with gold braid, perhaps a variation of naval officer's uniform. His white silk stockings show a distinctive wide rib and are probably hand knitted*

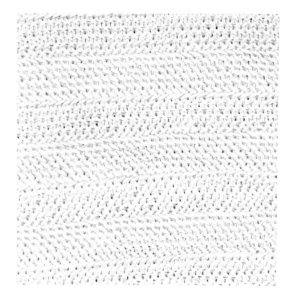

16 *Detail of knotted work in white silk, from a stocking of 1780–1800. The play of light on the diagonal threads gives the appearance of a rib when the rows are vertical*

Knotted stockings became popular for a while. By 1795 a thousand frames had difficulty in meeting the demand, but by 1805 only fifty frames were making them. In the 1790s William Gardiner, a Leicester hosier, met Daniel Lambert, the phenomenally large man who died in Stamford in 1809 aged thirty six and weighing 52 stones. 'I recollect he expressed to me the great difficulty he had in procuring stockings large enough. There was at that time a newly invented stocking called 'knotted hose', which was wrought lengthways upon the frame; I put him upon wearing these, as they could be made of any width.'[11] A pair of white silk stockings are preserved with other items of Lambert's wardrobe at the Newarke Houses Museum, Leicester. His calf measured forty inches round, too large for anything which could be made on the standard frame.

Horton's success encouraged imitations. William Brockley, of Nottingham, made twilled or plated stockings in 1776 in which 'the web lost its looped appearance and assumed a twilled face. By removing the twilled stitches to the right or left, a kind of stripe might be attained.'[12] They were, however, non-elastic. By using two threads

in alternate rows he made stockings which were silk on the outside and cotton inside. 'These were not inaptly called plated stockings, and became extensively in demand, as a low priced slop [ready-made] article, in imitation of knotted stockings; but their want of elasticity was ever a great drawback in their consumption, notwithstanding the general use of them, for their beauty.'[13] The Dutch magazine *Kabinet van Mode en Smaak* in 1792 described an Englishman as wearing 'violet and white striped stockings; with silk worked on a cotton ground. These kind of stockings are cheap, wear well and look good.'[14]

Robert Ash, also of Nottingham, made a better imitation by adding a wire to the tickler apparatus used by Brockley. His stockings were elastic but coarse and found a market in the Spanish and Portuguese colonies.[15] Samuel Hague patented an improvement of the machine in 1790 (No.1777) and collaborated with John Eaton on another frame. The products of his, Eaton's and Ash's frames had more stretch than the twilled hose and were called 'elastics'.[16]

Imitation ribs were also made on the warp frame, invented in about 1775. It worked on a new principle, combining the vertical warps of the weaving loom with the loops of the stocking frame. To interconnect the vertical rows of loops, guides shifted the thread from one needle, where it looped, to the next needle for the following row, and back again for the subsequent row, looping at each change of position. The threads crossing diagonally between rows gave the fabric a twilled appearance. Stockings made on this machine were also made horizontally and unfortunately were so inelastic that their seams were apt to burst even while being put on.[17] In silk they barely lasted a season as a fashion but of cotton they proved popular in Germany. In colour and with the thread passing across the space of more than one needle a zigzag stripe could be produced. These were called 'Vandyke warps' either from the zigzag points on the falling collars in Vandyke's portraits or after one of the putative inventors of the warp frame.[18] Occasionally zigzag stripes are seen on men's stockings in prints and paintings, such as Boilly's *Point de Convention* (about 1801) or Vernet's *Les*

Incroyables (1797).[19] A brightly coloured pair of stockings with a zigzag stripe is in the collection of Leicester Museums, and has been variously dated to 1755–75 and the late nineteenth century, but might well belong to the 1790s.[20]

Plain stripes appear more often and are virtually a cliché in the caricatures of Macaroni dress of the 1770s, although in written descriptions they do not figure prominently. Macaronis were men of fashion who had visited Italy as part of their education but, as a description of style, referred to a small hat, hair in a thick roll below the nape of the neck, a tight sleeved coat which sloped away in front, a very short waistcoat and low cut shoes. According to *The Town and Country Magazine* in 1772 they wore wide striped breeches and 'their legs are at times covered with all the colours of the rainbow; even flesh coloured and green silk stockings are not excluded. Their shoes are scarce slippers, and their buckles are within an inch of the toe.'[21] More waspishly *The Macaroni Magazine* describes the shoes 'cut like a butterboat to show the clocks of the stockings'.[22] A young man in Leicester wore a black collared light grey coat with silver cord buttons, diamond knee and shoe buckles and 'sky-blue ribbed silk stockings' to a ball in the late 1780s or early 1790s.[23]

Striped, diced and banded stockings

Ribbed and imitation ribbed hose continued in fashion until the end of the century though the width of the rib or stripe varied considerably. It was broad in the 1780s. French fashion plates, such as those in the *Galerie des Modes* of 1787 show stripes an inch or so wide. They are described as 'English Stockings' which could mean that they were imported or that they were in English style, as English fashions were very fashionable in France just before the Revolution. An improvement of the 'Derby Rib' apparatus, patented in 1784, was taken to France by a Frenchman, Rhamboldt, in about 1790.[24]

17 Stocking with zigzag pattern in red, green, black, blue and yellow silk; 1790–1800, made on the warp frame. Length 23½ inches, foot length 8 inches

The stripes were narrower in the 1790s. The Victoria and Albert Museum has a pair of blue striped white stockings which seem to date from this decade.[25] They have a twilled surface and are rather inelastic so are probably either 'twilled' or warp frame; it being almost impossible to tell the difference. The plain black and plain white silk stockings with narrow stripes which survive in a number of museum collections are probably either twilled or warp frame also, but the wider stripes are probably 'knotted' especially if they stretch.

Broad ribbed stockings in 1786 were also described as having 'stripes either horizontal or perpendicular'. The combination of a wide rib with bands of two different colours alternately would give a pattern of squares. These might be the 'diced' stockings which were worn in the first half of the eighteenth century but were

18 *Lilac silk stocking with lace clock and embroidery, 1785–1800; welt with six lozenges of nine holes. Length 26 inches, foot length 9 inches, 40 stitches per inch, 45 rows per vertical inch*

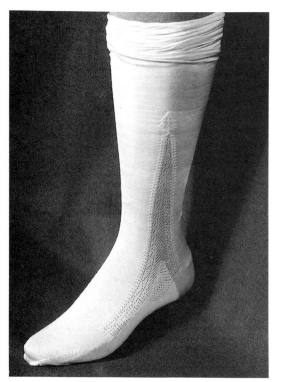

particularly fashionable for men in the 1760s. In a memorandum for 6 April 1763 James Boswell noted: 'then dress in a frock suit and five shilling diced stockings and clean shirt, and sally at three to Sheridan's.'[26] A black silk stocking of the 1840s in the Museum of Costume and Textiles, Nottingham, shows another method of making squares: every tenth row is a slack row and the vertical stripes are made by removing or isolating every tenth needle.[27]

Banded or horizontally striped hose seem to have also become popular in the 1790s. 'Jessamies', the successors of the Macaronis, wore deep bands in 1790. They inspired the Incroyables of the French Directory period. In *Le Petit Coblentz*, a watercolour by J B Isabey, the men are wearing either horizontally banded or vertically striped stockings.[28] Bands, being plain knitted and easy to make, continued in production past the turn of the century.

A further method of achieving a stripe was to use the ordinary stocking frame and a thread carrier invented in the 1770s.[29] This was operated by a treadle to lay two differently coloured threads in stripes. The stripes would be plain knitted but linked together by a technique known as 'intarsia'. The thread carrier has been described as the most important apparatus applied to the stocking frame. It seems to have been first used for making silk mittens.

Lace clocks and chevening

Frame knitted gloves and mittens with openwork patterns made by hand transference of loops from one needle to another had been imported from Spain from as early as 1700.[30] A mid century slump encouraged hosiers to look for novelties and in the 1760s various attempts to make an openwork fabric led first to lace clocks and then to machine-made lace.

In 1764 John Morris, a Nottingham hosier, patented a combination of tuck presser, Derby Rib apparatus and double-eyed ticklers, which had been the invention of two men, Butterworth and Betts. The ticklers acted on the needles and, by being given a sideways motion, helped to transfer the loops from one needle to another and make eyelet holes or network. Arthur Else doubled the speed of the machine by using single-eyed ticklers alone but infringed the patent. Morris prosecuted, won and appropriated his machine. In 1769 Robert Frost added a preselection device, a carved wooden roller whose projections acted on slide lever ticklers to make a pattern. Examples of his lace survive at Nottingham but it is not certain that his device was used for stockings.

Lace clocks proved popular particularly with women. The most favoured style was wide in the base and sometimes extended down the side of the foot to make a V on the instep, fitting into the pointed throat of fashionable shoes. By 1783 frameworkers making lace clocks and their colleagues making knotted, twilled and elastic hose were earning from 18s to 30s per week. Makers of plain hose with long clocks received between 10s to 14s per week.[31]

Both plain and lace clocks could also be embellished with embroidery or 'chevening', introduced or invented by Mrs Elizabeth (Bess) Drake, a stocking seamer, in 1783.[32] Chevening was smaller in scale and more closely related to the stitches in the stocking than earlier embroidery. It could be in the same or a contrasting colour, in silk on silk or wool, or glazed linen on cotton. The designs were the stylised flowers, trees and crowns already familiar from earlier clocks. Silk stockings with wide clocks embroidered in the traditional manner with flowers and birds are thought to be Spanish imports. Towards the end of the century silk itself suffered increasing competition from fine cotton.

Cotton stockings

In 1688–9 Robert Graham, tailor, charged 18s for making six pairs of white silk drawers and 'sowing fine cotton stockings to them' for William III.[33] The stockings, which were presumably under-stockings, might have come from Thomas Styles and partners who supplied thirty six pairs of cotton hose, four pairs of grey hose and three pairs of Holland hose in that year.[34] Celia Fiennes noted the spinning of cotton and the knitting of

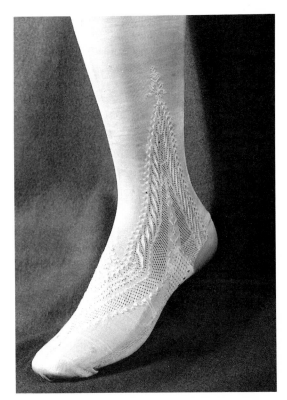

19   Cream silk stocking with embroidered lace clock, 1790–1810; marked 'C' below the welt. Length 23¼ inches, foot length 8¼ inches, 40 stitches per inch, 50 rows per vertical inch

it into stockings, gloves, waistcoats, petticoats and sleeves in Gloucester in 1698.[35] The cotton was imported from India into Gloucester and Bristol and spun and knitted principally around Evesham, Worcestershire. The short cotton fibres were like the local wool and were spun by hand or wheel: as early as 1699 there is mention of a 'Cotton Wheel' in a household inventory.[36] Up to the 1740s these stockings appear to have been hand knitted and utilitarian rather than fashionable, worn perhaps in summer in preference to worsted as both had a matt surface, whereas glossy linen thread was a substitute for silk. Fine cotton stockings could also have been hand knitted from imported Indian cotton yarn.

In the 1740s stocking frames were introduced into Tewkesbury, one of the centres of cotton knitting.[37] The first frame-knitted stockings had been made of expensive Indian cotton on a 20

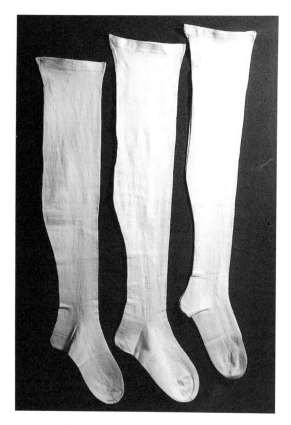

20 *Cotton stockings shown by J R Allen at the Great Exhibition, 1851, originally labelled:*
Left: *'5 thread, 34 gauge Hose, Made in the Year 1790, cotton spun by Sir R Arkwright'. Length 27½ inches, foot length 10½ inches, 34 stitches per inch, 39 rows per vertical inch. Marked 'I'*
Centre: *'2 Threads, 26 Gauge Hose, Made in the Year 1804, From Cotton spun by Mr R Arkwright'. Length 29¼ inches, foot length 10½ inches, 26 stitches per inch, 30 rows per vertical inch*
Right: *'2 Threads, 38 Gauge Hose, Made in the Year 1810, from cotton spun by Mr R Arkwright'. Length 27¼ inches, foot length 10¼ inches, 38 stitches per inch, 45 rows per vertical inch. Marked 'S 70', two pink lines on welt*

gauge silk frame in Nottingham in 1730.[38] The number of framework knitters grew in Tewkesbury in the 1750s and 1760s and the Nottingham knitters became increasingly jealous, as the spinners of the East Midlands, used to the long staple wool of Leicestershire sheep, could not cope with the short fibre. Tewkesbury cotton hose undersold Nottingham ones made of Indian yarn by a quarter of the price and did not wear so well. Largely as a result of Nottingham's representations an act, later known as the 'Tewkesbury Act' was hurried through Parliament in 1765.[39] By this act all stockings made of thread, cotton, worsted or yarn, alone or mixed, except pure silk, which combined three or more threads twisted together, had to be marked with a row of holes, one hole for each thread. Unfortunately the act omitted to cover all hose made of two threads doubled together, and as manufacturers marked stockings with three, four or five holes, even when made of two threads, the act speedily became a dead letter. However, some manufacturers found the holes sufficiently useful to indicate quality and continued to use them. Even late nineteenth century stockings can be found with rows of holes on or below the welt and on the heel or sole. Notwithstanding the act Tewkesbury frameworkers flourished. By the early nineteenth century they were selling women's super, extra super and super super (38 gauge) stockings, plain, embroidered or with clocks; maids' (girls') stockings in a similar range; men's ribbed and plain, slender to outsize; stockings for children; socks for both sexes, and pantaloon drawers. But by 1816 the Tewkesbury industry was in decline, largely because good quality machine spun cotton was being produced in Nottingham.[40]

Lewis Paul patented a machine for spinning cotton in 1738.[41] The first experiments were made in Birmingham and a hank of cotton exists spun in 1741 by a machine powered by two mules. Further improvements were made in 1758, but the thread was unsuitable for hosiery. The fact that cotton could be spun inspired other inventors. In Blackburn James Hargreaves invented a jenny to spin more than one thread at a time, but local spinners, fearful for their livelihoods, forced him to move in 1768 to Nottingham where, in Mill Street, he built a small factory and patented his device.[42] Unfortunately it was pirated and he received no monetary benefit. Richard Arkwright, a barber from Preston, likewise received no encouragement from Lancashire for an invention of spinning with rollers and moved to Nottingham where he built a factory in Hockley.[43] By 1775 he was to spin a smooth thread suitable for hosiery. The Rivers Leen and Trent could not provide enough motive power and he moved to Cromford, Derbyshire, where the force of the Derwent was sufficient to turn a waterwheel. With Jedediah Strutt he built a mill at Belper and when the partnership dissolved in 1781 he retained the Cromford mill, and Strutt the mills at Belper and Milford.[44]

By great good fortune a series of stockings exists which shows the progress of Arkwright's cotton thread from 1790, through 1804, and 1810, to 1826.[45] They are part of a collection of hose and half-hose which William Felkin noticed at the International Exhibition in 1862, but which, in fact, had been shown at the Great Exhibition in 1851 and probably at an exhibition in Nottingham in 1840.[46] The collection had been formed by J R Allen (1793–1868), a hosier, of St James's Street, Nottingham. Ten of these stockings have hand-written labels probably original to the display, and written well within Allen's lifetime. They provide rare instances of dated stockings. Other than the threads used there is little about them that is remarkable. The turn shape decoration is so slight that it is practically invisible from a distance, but it does seem to be typical of its period. Guy Head's portrait of Admiral Nelson, painted between 1798 and 1800, shows him in matt white stockings with the same slight decoration at the ankles.[47]

The fine spinning achieved by Arkwright's machines meant that cotton stockings became very fashionable. Even though England and France were at war the Empress Josephine asked for, and got, six pairs of cotton stockings from England.[48] It was William Gardiner's opinion that had the Peace of Amiens (1802) continued for longer, English fortunes would have been made from the export of silk point net and cotton stockings. 'No articles were so highly esteemed as English ladies' cotton stockings. Their peculiar whiteness and fineness recommended them as preferable to silk, and they sold for higher prices.'[49] Not that they entirely ousted silk. On

the return from a trip to Paris in 1802 Gardiner was attracted to a vivacious lady in the coach, but she horrified him by arriving for dinner at Calais in 'dark purple silk stockings with staring yellow clocks and yellow silk shoes.'[50] He made a hurried excuse and left for England immediately.

Silk stockings in fashion

References to the wearing of silk stockings by both sexes in the second half of the eighteenth century are numerous. Women wore either white or black, usually the former. Even when the skirt rose to just above the ankles in the 1750s and 1780s, the stocking thus revealed is very rarely anything other than white. But white could have coloured clocks. James Fitzgerald, 20th Earl of Kildare, in London in 1762 wrote to his wife that he had 'bespoke two pairs with bright blue, two pairs with green, and two pairs with pink coloured clocks, all different patterns and will wash very well. I will bespoke [sic] you six pairs more with white clocks; you mean to have them embroidered I suppose, therefore I shall order them so'.[51] The order was ready in ten days. Brides, as one might expect, wore white. A young married lady who died in 1763 was buried in her wedding clothes which included white silk stockings and silver spangled shoes. Her white negligée (or sack-back dress) and petticoat were quilted to make the coffin lining.[52] White was even usual for mourning until 1778 when Mrs Damer, the sculptor, and an eccentric, introduced black silk stockings for ladies' wear.[53] Silk stockings were expensive. Lord and Lady Middleton paid £1 17s for two pairs of silk hose from a Nottingham hosier, Samuel Hepper in 1799, and in 1807 the enormous sum of £24 12s 6d for silk stockings from Thomas Newton of Derby but the quantity is not specified nor is the length of time the bill had been running.[54] By this date Derby was established as a centre for silk stocking production, largely due to the silk throwing mill of Sir Thomas Lombe, established in 1718, and by the 1730s producing organzine silk to rival Italy. Nottingham was the centre for cotton hosiery and Leicester for wool, but, in fact, all three types of stocking were made in each town.

White silk stockings were commonly worn by men too, even in the day. Jack Chace in Francis Coventry's novel _Pompey the Little_ (1753) wore them with green, red or blue collared Newmarket frocks, and buckskin breeches and carried a whip.[55] In Paris in June 1790 they were suggested wear with a sky-blue collared velvet coat, an orange casimir waistcoat and an ornamental dagger-stick.[56] In the Netherlands the next year they were worn with a high black felt hat, 'Vandyked' neck-cloth, grey-yellow cloth coat, white waistcoat, dark blue breeches and a Herculean club![57] They were particularly worn with full dress, indeed at some places – assembly rooms and opera houses – boots were banned and shoes had to be worn with silk stockings. In England white silk stockings were worn equally with a black coat or dark blue frock, white waistcoat and black breeches (foreshadowing nineteenth-century evening dress) in 1782, as with a puce velvet coat, green rose-checked waistcoat and black satin breeches in

1786.[58] Footmen, as personal servants, were sometimes given silk stockings to wear. In the mid 1760s John Macdonald was given a dozen pairs of silk stockings by his new master John Crauford of Errol who told him 'I like my servants to go genteelly'.[59] Superior London tradesmen also wore white silk stockings, even with the apron of their calling, and John Howard, a retired London upholsterer still clung to white silk stockings in the country, when wool would have been more appropriate.[60]

Silk stockings were given the tenderest care. The housemaid might mend her master's common stockings but only the housekeeper might mend his silk ones.[61] If worn or stained at the feet, they could be refooted or dyed, at a cost of 3s per pair in 1757.[62]

21 Plate from 'Neues Nah und Strictbuch fur das schone Geschlecht...' [New needlework and knitting book for the fair sex], 1784. The star and crown, by now a traditional motif, is similar to the turn shape star and crown in the 1790 stocking in plate 20

Worsted stockings

Worsted stockings were worn by all classes. In general the upper classes wore machine knitted ones as being finer. The lower classes were more likely to wear coarser hand-knitted hose, although some fine hand-knitted stockings were produced in places such as Aberdeen. Brown or blue stockings of home spun and knitted yarn were worn by South Lancashire working men with low crowned, broad-brimmed hats, blue or drab woollen or fustian jackets and leather breeches.[63] In the middle of the century the Duke of Bedford supplied his footmen with worsted stockings and other clothes for rough work.[64] Mr Briggs, a merchant, in Fanny Burney's novel *Cecilia* (1782) habitually wore a snuff coloured suit and blue and white speckled stockings.[65] In Bedfordshire John Blundell's sister knitted him stockings using 11 to 12 ounces of grey or speckled wool per pair in the 1760s. He himself paid 5s 6d for a pair of ribbed stockings at the Shillington Statute Fair in 1764.[66] In 1797 in Cumberland 11 ounces of wool at 8d the pound was the average amount for a pair of stockings; a locally made suit cost £1 12s 3d. Leicestershire yeomen wore light grey worsted hose with short drab coats and red waistcoats to the races, but many portraits of the middle-aged or elderly show stockings matching the suit.

Women's worsted stockings, like their silk ones, were often black or white. The women of South Lancashire, for instance, wore blue flannel bedgowns, aprons and petticoats, white mob-caps and hand-knitted stockings of black or white yarn. White stockings with blue clocks, printed cotton gowns, and black beaver hats were worn by the female guests at a wedding in Caernarvon in 1796. Women's hand-knitted stockings in Cumberland in 1797 were valued at 1s 8d the pair. In 1789 Mrs Papiendieck stated: 'Black worsted stockings [are] now only seen on servants of an inferior order and the lower working classes'.[67] In 1793 Lady Pamela Fitzgerald, a fashion conscious Frenchwoman, created a sensation at a Dublin ball by wearing black stockings with red clocks, and a black dress trimmed with 'Cocklico' (probably coquelicot, a bright scarlet) ribbons, which were considered to be Jacobin colours. 'She was at the Rotunda Ball some nights ago and in a strange attire, with black and scarlet ribbons bound in ye sandal way over her stockings, which the shortness of her petticoat and extraordinary movement of kicking in dancing made very visible. The company (some of the grandest in Dublin) star'd at her with so much curiosity that she went away crying.'[68]

Coloured clocks

Coloured clocks were fleetingly fashionable for both sexes in 1776, and gold clocks in 1785, but whether these were embroidered or gore clocks there is no indication. German pattern books from 1748 to 1817 include embroidery patterns of stylised crowns and flowers, some of which are adaptable to chevening or plating. Plating was a machine technique of laying a pattern thread in front of the base thread and knitting the two together. The pattern appeared on the face but not on the reverse of the stocking. In England this technique appears to have been abandoned by 1750: 'hose embroidered by the insertion of threads forming a pattern by hand, while the stocking was in process of manufacture had ceased to be made'.[69] In other countries this technique may have continued. In the records of the Poneggen Castle enterprise in Austria there is a reference to two stocking frames producing three-thread woollen stockings with a floral pattern. The pattern was probably the clock, and also, since there is no indication that it was a separate process, made by turn shapes or plating.

European and American stocking knitting and trade

The Poneggen enterprise was set up with imperial support in 1764 to provide work for a growing population and to reduce the number of imports, particularly from North Germany.[70] Most of the stockings were wool, hand knitted in the area around the Castle, made, finished and marketed according to regulations which still survive and give an unusually detailed picture of hosiery production in the second half of the eighteenth century. A wide range of plain and patterned stockings was made for men, women and boys, principally in blue for men, red for women, but also in brown, black, silver, corn, green, dark coffee, medium green and 'nacra' (pearl coloured). Striped stockings were produced from 1784. In terms of quantity the enterprise was a success. By 1765 it had a stock of seven hundred dozen pairs of stockings and the three directors were asking for an increase in import duties. But in fineness the stockings could not rival those of Hamburg. Between 1767 and 1779 it was granted a monopoly and regulated the import of four varieties of women's stockings from Hamburg as well as hose from Kaunitz, Reichenberg and Dux. After 1779 when it lost the monopoly it started to go downhill and in 1818 it closed.

The Poneggen Castle enterprise was only one part of a great trade in stockings at the end of the eighteenth century. Large quantities of mostly hand-knitted stockings were shipped to almost all parts of the world with here and there attempts to set up manufacturing concerns. Aberdeen, a centre of a hand-knitting industry with a few stocking frames, exported to Rotterdam, Poland, Berghen, Compvere (Veer on the island of Walcheren), and Virginia.[71] Aberdeen stockings were generally white, and sold in 1747 for between 30s and £4 a pair.[72] Nîmes in France, was exporting over two million pairs of stockings to Spain and Southern Europe with more than two and three-quarter million pairs of silk, cotton, and wool hose to Switzerland, Germany, Northern Europe and within France itself. These were the products of 5,100 stocking frames.[73] In 1746 the first frames were set up in Troyes in the lower Champagne region of France. These frames and others in the villages around Troyes and Romilly-sur-Seine provided small farmers with a welcome additional source of income.[74]

In America there were 150 frames in Germantown and Philadelphia before 1775 upon which brown and white thread and cotton hosiery was made, advertised in 1789 as cheaper and more lasting 'than those of any nation in Europe'. Colonel Christopher Leffingwell established a stocking factory at Norwich, Connecticut, in 1771 and within a few years there were frames at Hartford, New Haven, Litchfield, and Wallingford, Connecticut and Poughkeepsie, New York. The War of Independence, by cutting off America from British imports, doubtless stimulated the industry. In 1776 Daniel Mause urged Americans through *The Pennsylvania Gazette* to be patriotic and buy his thread and cotton stockings. By 1778 Norwich was producing silk and worsted as well as cotton and thread stockings.[75]

Varieties of stockings

By the end of the eighteenth century, even before the era of the large scale factory, there was a sizeable export-import trade in stockings, yet it was still an era of individuality. Stockings were one-off in pattern, subject to fashion, and the individual quirks of the knitter and wearer. Some idea of the range of available stockings can be gained from the diary of the Reverend James Woodforde, vicar of a parish in Norfolk, and from an inventory of clothing compiled by Samuel Curwen, a merchant of Salem, Massachusetts, while he was in England in 1780.[76] Parson Woodforde, like most clergymen, wore black silk stockings for best at 12s to 14s 6d a pair, or a cotton and silk mixture at 8s 6d. He had coarse and fine ribbed stockings, fine black and white stockings, 'ash-coloured welch stockings' and coursing stockings knitted with wool straight off the sheep's back to keep out the wet. When afflicted with the gout in the 1790s he wore both white lambswool knitted stockings and worsted gauze ones. Curwen had thirty nine pairs of stockings, most of them of silk, which were variously white mottled, black and blue striped, speckled blue, purple and white speckled, dark mottled and black. His silk and worsted mixture hose were brown and black and white. Sadly, this great wealth is not reflected in the few surviving eighteenth-century stockings.

4

1800–60

Between 1812 and 1844 there was a great upsurge in the number of stocking frames in the Midlands region. In Leicestershire the number rose from 11,173 to 20,861, in Nottinghamshire from 9,285 to 16,382 and in Derbyshire from 4,700 to 6,797.[1] Except in Scotland, where the number of frames in work had risen by 37 per cent to 1,985, this increase was not reflected elsewhere in the United Kingdom. In 1812 there had been 2,965 frames in Ireland and the rest of England; by 1844 this number had decreased to 1,225. The rise in the number of the frames and their concentration in the Midlands was due to a combination of factors. A boom in stocking production following the ending of the American War in 1783 encouraged over-investment in frames. A slump, inflation during the Napoleonic wars, bad harvests and a rise in population meant that, as more people turned to the frame as an alternative source of income, there was not sufficient work to keep them all fully occupied. The result was great hardship and near starvation for all but a handful of stockingers from about 1810 until 1850. From relative affluence in the late eighteenth century many descended to scraping an existence, subsisting off bread and potatoes, supplemented in extreme cases by opium, or opium-laced Godfrey's cordial for the children.[2] In bad years such as 1812 and 1819 there were heavy calls on parish relief, and public appeals for help. In January 1812 half the population of Nottingham was unemployed, and relieved from the Poor Rates.[3]

This period also saw, on the one hand, the rise of dynastic hosiers, founders of firms which would continue into the present century, and, on the other hand, an increase in bag-hosiers, the middle men, and in various fraudulent practices detrimental to the trade.

The dynastic hosiers and their firms

In 1797 John Morley established himself in Russia Row, London, as the selling end of the manufacturing business set up by his brother Richard in Nottingham. The firm of I [the eighteenth century version of J] and R Morley was born.[4] Similarly, John Ward took premises in Cateaton Street, London, selling the products of his family's business in Belper.[5] In 1803 this firm became Ward, Brettle and Ward and by the 1820s was possibly the largest hosiery manufacturer in the country. In 1834 it split into George Brettle & Co and Ward, Sturt, Sharp & Ward. The latter as Ward, Sturt & Sharp continued into the 1930s, and the former was acquired by Courtaulds in 1964. Allen, Solly & Co Ltd started as Allen & Phillips in 1809, becoming successively John Allen & Sons in 1818, Allen, Solly & Allen in 1832, Allen & Solly in 1835, Allen, Solly & Co in 1860, and a limited company in 1912. By 1848 a London office had been acquired, also property in Godalming, Surrey, another framework knitting centre. In the 1950s it became part of the Viyella International Federation of Companies. Nathaniel Corah started business in 1815, buying from stockingers in Leicester and selling in Birmingham. In 1830 his sons joined him in the business and in 1845 they began manufacturing on steam driven frames in Granby Street, Leicester. Their more famous factory, St Margaret's Works was opened in 1865 and N Corah & Sons, a limited company since 1919, celebrated its centenary in 1965.[6]

Marks

In the late eighteenth and early nineteenth

centuries many major firms started to mark their products with one or more initials worked into the knitting usually on or just below the welt. This helped to identify a firm's goods when an independent knitter might work for more than one hosier, and acted as a guarantee of quality to the purchaser. The earliest dated marked stocking which can be linked to a firm is one of 1826 in the J R Allen Collection at Nottingham. It has 'A' for John Allen & Sons. There is another stocking, of 1790, in the same collection which is marked 'I' but this can be only tentatively connected with the Illingworth of Amys, Allen & Illingworth (1783–1805), of Nottingham. There are records of earlier identifying marks. King Charles X Gustavus of Sweden's stockings in the mid seventeenth century have an 'I' or a 'C' knitted in.[7] Between 1754 and 1774 English framework knitters worked 'PARIS' below the welt of stockings to pass them off as the better quality French hose.[8] (The same mark was used on Parisian made cotton stockings in the 1840s.) In 1755 gentlemen and ladies might 'have their own name wrought in the stocking whilst weaving' and in 1804 William Gardiner sent Joseph Haydn in Vienna six pairs of cotton stockings with quotations from that composer's works in the actual knitting.[9] Sadly they never reached him. Royal stockings are usually marked

with an openwork crown above a cipher, 'VR' for Queen Victoria, 'AR' for Queen Adelaide and so forth, though sometimes the crown and cipher are embroidered.

Marks at the Poneggen Castle factory in Austria were tied to quality control.[10] According to regulations in 1771 each frameworker and hand knitter had to mark their products, the latter so as 'to enable the company to hold him responsible for bad work'. Small initials inside the welt are often those of the actual frameworker or commissioning agent, but the large initials below the welt are usually those of a firm, at least in England. I & R Morley used an 'M', Allen, Solly & Co in its various name changes, an 'A' and 'A...A' between 1832 and 1835, and George Brettle & Co a 'B'. 'W' might be for Ward, Sturt, Sharp & Ward. 'C' which appears on a number of late eighteenth and early nineteenth century stockings, might be Cooke's Manufactory and Nottingham Warehouse, 434 Strand, London, but there were quite a number of Nottingham and London hosiers with names beginning with 'C'. 'G.R.' might be George Ray & Co of Friar Lane, Nottingham, and 141 Gutter Lane, London. Corah of Leicester used 'NC' or 'N.C & S' at least from 1862; and Stephen Elliott of Swanwick, Derbyshire an 'E', from the 1870s. In the first half of the century numbers were sometimes used, knitted into the welts, these, though some are in the thousands, are thought to refer to identifying numbers on frames.

Marked hosiery was only a small proportion of what was actually produced. Cotton and worsted plain hose, and cotton, worsted and thread ribbed hose were the most common products with a much smaller number of plain and ribbed silk hose. Silk knotted and elastic hose were still being made in 1812. The commonest types were made for bag hosiers, the village middlemen, who supplied the materials and sold on the finished products, working on slender profit margins and paying, when they could get away with it, by 'truck', that is, by goods instead of money.

Poor trade led to fraudulent practices: the theft of yarn by using only one thread instead of two or more, the soaping of silk to make it

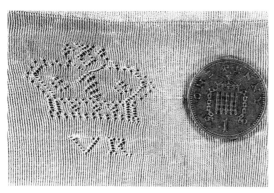

22 *Crown and initials made by transferring stitches by hand, from a pair of very fine pink silk stockings made for Queen Victoria, 1840–50; they are as sheer as a modern nylon stocking. Similar stockings were buried in time capsules under foundation stones in Nottingham from the 1840s to the 1870s and have been recovered on demolition. 48 stitches per inch, 80 rows per vertical inch*

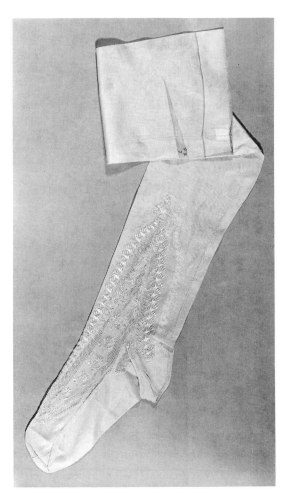

23 Fine white silk stocking with embroidered lace clock, 1810–25; pink lines at the edges of the welt, mark '919' on welt; though of very high quality, the absence of the crown above the V R suggests that they did not belong to Queen Victoria. Length 23¼ inches, foot length 7½ inches, 56 stitches per inch

Fashion and stockings

In the difficulties of the hosiery trade fashion played its part. The muslin gown which had developed from the chemise à la reine, worn by Queen Marie Antoinette of France in the 1780s, was now a general fashion, at once democratic, as muslin was readily available, and classical, harking back to the golden ages of Greece and Rome, while contemporary politics, particularly in France, were in turmoil. Beneath the muslin little else was worn, at least by the young and fashionable. 'The fashion for false bosoms has at least this utility; that it compels our fashionable fair to wear something' (1799).[12] 'The only sign of modesty in the present dress of the ladies is the pink dye in their stockings, which makes their legs appear to blush for the total absence of petticoats' (1803).[13] Tight tubes of stockinet were worn as petticoats in the early years of the century over conventional stockings but in 1812 Cooke's Manufactory and Nottingham Warehouse, in London, was selling pantaloon-drawers with feet and ladies' underdresses all in one.[14]

Brooks & Co of Nottingham and Derby, reflected the uncertainty of the times by offering silk, cotton and worsted hose 'in any quantity not less than three pairs, for ready money' at their London warehouse. In 1812 they reassured their customers 'that their frames at Nottingham and its vicinity are all at work, and their mechanics peaceable without exception'; but as there was no export trade they were offering their hose at 20 per cent discount.[15] Jane Austen paid 12s a pair for silk stockings in 1811 at Grafton House, a fashionable London emporium, and despite waiting for half-an-hour to be served, was well pleased with her purchase.[16] Cooke's Manufactory and Nottingham Warehouse advertised stockings in stout cotton at 1s 6d a pair, in black or coloured worsted at 1s 3d, and in black or white silk at 6s 6d in 1811 and 1812.[17] These silk stockings were probably either quite plain or with triangular openwork clocks surrounded by hand embroidery. Some have a pattern in the net work and they might be the 'silk stockings with lace clocks, richly brocaded' worn with kid slippers for morning dress in

weigh heavier, and 'cut ups'. Knotted, twilled, plated, and warp frame hose, being made across the frame, had always been cut and seamed. Now the technique extended to cutting the stocking from a rectangle of stockinet made on the wide frame. Despite the extra process involved this was cheaper than shaping each stocking individually on the frame and led to lower prices. One of the chief aims of the frame smashing activities of the Luddites between 1811 and 1815 was to put a stop to 'cut ups'.[11]

1812.[18] Wide based triangular clocks are notice-able in the caricatures of the period. The embroidery could be in the colour of the stocking or in a colour, pink, blue or green, on white. Black stockings were always embroidered in black. Few have survived, as the acid in perspiration accelerated the disintegration of the black dye.

Other colours were worn. Pink gave an illusion of nudity. Mary Boyle Harvey and her Irish sister-in-law wore flesh-coloured silk stockings with thin silk dresses, white kid shoes and gauze neckerchiefs at a wedding in Cork in June 1809.[19] Walking stockings, perhaps of a heavier weight, in brown, grey or olive coloured silk with yellow clocks were worn in 1802,[20] the same year that William Gardiner encountered purple stockings with yellow clocks.

During the Napleonic Wars silk was scarce in England as most of it was imported from territories in enemy hands. Manufacturers concentrated on providing a finer thread spun from Indian and Egyptian cottons. In 1805 Samuel Cartledge introduced a very fine cotton thread to the Nottingham lace trade when machine lace was still being made on adapted stocking frames.[21] A much smoother thread was obtained by 'gassing', the passing of the thread through a gas flame to singe off stray fibres. Samuel Hall of Nottingham patented the process in 1817.[22] His father, Robert Hall, introduced chloride of lime as a bleach for cotton hosiery threads and invented 'angola' yarn (a mixture of animal and cotton fibres) for stockings. Cooke's advertised Angola drawers in 1812. Consequently England, and in particular Nottingham, led the way in the making of fine, smooth, cotton stockings. In 1815 French ladies preferred fine India cotton stockings from England to silk hose from Paris.[23] By 1822 openwork cotton stockings were generally worn unless the dress was silk and then silk stockings were appropriate.[24]

Women's magazines, such as *The Ladies' Monthly Museum*, made more reference to silk stockings than to cotton ones, in their rather skimpy fashion reportage. However, as the severe classicism of female dress was modified the fashion reports became more verbose and the number of magazines increased. *La Belle*

Assemblée, founded in 1806, and *The World of Fashion*, started in 1824, to name but two, had better quality fashion plates in which the fashion in stockings can be seen, as well as followed in the text.

The classical dress lost its train for all but formal occasions from about 1805 in England, earlier in France. The skirt rose and became short and full, particularly for evening dress, in about 1815 or 1816. The waist was still high under the bust and, although it fluctuated, it reached its natural level in the mid 1820s. Decoration appeared at the top of the arms and at the skirt hem where it drew attention to neat ankles in openwork stockings. Shoes, until the 1820s were still pointed at the toe and throat, and the decoration on the stocking followed this line or continued round the front of the foot. It rarely rose above the lower calf. Some stockings, particularly from the 1830s have a French or sandal foot, with the seam under the foot rather than at the sides. This looked more elegant in a low-cut shoe.

From 1827 *élégantes* wore shoes and stockings to match: ethereal blue silk stockings and blue kid slippers with a 'blush taffety' carriage dress, for instance, or white silk stockings and white shoes embroidered with gold to match the embroidery on a gold lamé or tulle dress.[25] Stockings with gold embroidery, this time lozenges on the instep, reappeared in 1829.[26] Other stockings had coloured embroidery but, in general, plain or openwork white or pale coloured silk was preferred for the evening. In January 1829 flesh coloured stockings were again fashionable, worn with checked satin shoes, and in December as part of a double act: 'Ladies who wish to have their feet well dressed, wear very fine stockings of open work; but, lest they should suffer from the cold, they have, underneath very long stockings of flesh colour, which serve as drawers, and are tied to the waist like those of children'.[27] Also in 1829 there was a welter of eccentric stocking fashions: flesh coloured silk woven with coloured flowers, or painted with butterflies and bluebirds, white silk with a harlequin, punchinello or devil climbing up a pine tree (at a masked ball), or brocaded

24 'La Valse', hand coloured French engraving, c 1800. The women wear white stockings with long narrow clocks embroidered in pink or green to match shoes and over and under-dresses respectively. Both men appear to wear pantaloons

over with Kashmiri flowers.[28] Some stockings imitated the knee high boot or were fringed above the ankle in imitation of the white silk half-boot fashionable for dancing.[29] Alternate stripes of plain and openwork were popular with printed cotton or silk dresses. At the beginning of the 1830s white silk stockings were worn with square toed black satin shoes for both day and evening. In 1835 the craze for blonde lace extended to the insteps of stockings.[30]

For walking dress, shoes and stockings matched, in dark, unobtrusive colours. Black stockings were worn only with black dresses. In mourning grey could be worn. Grey silk stock-

ings with embroidered black clocks were fashionable in November 1828, perhaps as a result of Court Mourning for George IV's sister, the Queen Dowager of Württemburg. They reappear together with similarly embroidered brown silk stockings in 1835 for country wear.[31] The embroidery on these stockings was probably slight, a satin stitch line with an arrowhead, flower, stylised tree or crown at the top. This style of decoration continued into the 1920s.

Gaiters

Where stockings were light coloured, the roads dusty or the weather inclement, gaiters of various materials and styles were worn: black with ivory buttons in 1825, grey or white, buttoned or laced to the knee for the fashionable Parisian pastime of donkey riding in September 1825.[32] A pair of gaiters of 1830–50 in white cotton

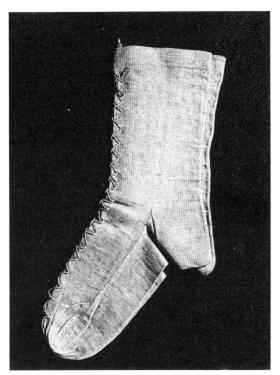

25   *Fawn cotton gaiters, shown at the Great Exhibition, 1851, by J R Allen; described on the original label 'Gaiters, made about the year 1812, cotton spun by Mr R Arkwright'; imitation lacing at the front. Length 10 inches, foot length 9¼ inches, 26 stitches per inch, 32 rows per vertical inch*

twill with lace to just below the knee is in the Gallery of English Costume.[33] A pair of brown cotton knitted pull-on gaiters with imitation lacing at the front is in the J R Allen Collection in Nottingham.[34] They are dated '*c* 1812'. A banded pair, perhaps later in date, is in the National Museum of Scotland, Edinburgh.[35] Both pairs were worn inside shoes. A caricature of Lord Byron abandoning his wife and child in 1816 shows both Lady Byron and her confidante in similar gaiters beneath short skirts.[36] Gaiters continued to be worn even after half-boots became fashionable in 1829.

Lisle stockings

In June 1829 stockings of Scotch thread were most in favour in Paris, and in 1835 day stockings of white or grey Lisle thread.[37] Scotch or Lisle thread was highly twisted and gassed cotton. In England it was used for gloves in Leicester in 1834, and probably for stockings about the same time.[38] Lisle thread was originally of linen from Lille in France; the cotton thread superseded it. From the mid nineteenth century 'thread' seems to mean cotton Lisle rather than linen, though flax was still spun for hosiery; J B & W Nevill & Co exhibited men's and women's white linen thread hose at the Great Exhibition in 1851.[39]

Two pairs of openwork stockings in the J R Allen Collection in Nottingham are probably of Lisle thread, the cotton is so very fine and smooth. Both pairs have the 'A...A' of the Allen, Solly & Allen partnership of 1832–5, and are decorated with openwork on the insteps, one pair with a three point zigzag top and leaves and sprigs embroidered in white in the openwork, the other with a central stem, openwork leaves, and delicate embroidery of oak foliage, acorns and roses in coloured silks.[40] The openwork patterns on these and other fine cotton hose in other collections were probably made by laboriously transferring each stitch by hand. For regular patterns some kind of pre-selection device, such as Robert Frost's carved wooden cylinder (1769 and 1780), or Dawson's wheels (1807) might have been used. During the 1830s attempts were made to adapt J M Jacquard's apparatus for weaving patterns on the draw-loom to the stocking frame. Jacquard had exhibited his device in 1800. It had cards punched with holes, one card per line of pattern, and a system of rods on strings which by falling through the holes or not dictated the movements of the loom. The growing interest in large bold patterns in the 1830s prompted inventors to adapt his apparatus to the lace making machines in Nottingham and the shawl weaving looms in Paisley, Scotland. In 1836 a Mr Cope of Radford, Nottingham built an eyelet hole stocking frame whose motions were governed by needles and perforated paper on the Jacquard principle and in 1841 a Mr Lupton, also of Radford, adapted the Jacquard to a tickler stocking frame.[41] Nevertheless many complex patterns would have been done by hand as labour was cheap. Some openwork stockings of the 1830s and 1840s, possibly even later, have another distinguishing feature, 'a twisted' back seam, which, when the stocking is flat, appears to veer to one side or the other, rather than going straight up the back. In wear it is indistinguishable from a true back seam. This 'twisted' seam does not appear to be a feature of a particular firm or place.

Openwork stockings were worn by all classes. In *Sketches by Boz* (Charles Dickens, 1836–7) Miss Jemima Evans, shoe binder and straw bonnet maker, wore them with a white muslin dress, red shawl and bonnet ribbons for an evening out with a journeyman carpenter. Agnes, a maidservant, wore them with a cherry coloured merino dress and shoes with sandals (ribbons crossed around the ankles and tied).[42] In *The Greatest Plague of Life; or a Lady in Search of a Good Servant* another maid, Susan, scandalised her mistress by dressing too fine in 'an imitation Balzarine gown of bright ultramarine, ringlets, a blonde lace cap with streamers, while on looking at her feet, if the conceited bit of goods hadn't got on patent leather shoes, with broad sandals, and open-worked cotton stockings'.[43]

Effects of fashion on women's stockings

By this time, the early 1840s, the skirt hem had reached the ground for most day and evening dresses. Skirts had been at their shortest in the late 1820s and early 1830s and, inevitably, had come in for much criticism. 'To affect wearing a dress excessively short, in order to display a well-turned ankle or a little foot, discovers a want of modesty ... How ridiculous are stockings when embroidered on the instep! Such coquetry can only find excuse from an opera dancer, who wishes to fix all the eyes of an audience on her legs and feet'.[44] The writer of this in 1829 doubtless welcomed the return of the long skirt in 1840, but it had serious consequences for the hosiery industry. In December 1839 the Marchioness of Normanby 'having heard that there is a present great distress in Nottingham from want of work' ordered from Barlow &

Comyn two dozen pairs of white silk stockings at 8s a pair for herself and a further six dozen on behalf of Queen Victoria'. The latter were to be marked with a crown, 'VR' and numbers up to 12. A stocking which survives with the Marchioness's letter, at the Ruddington Framework Knitters Trust in Nottinghamshire, is very fine with fifty six stitches to the inch. The clock is an embroidered line surmounted by a crown.

John Withers Taylor, manager of the silk department of Ward, Sturt & Sharp of Belper, was in no doubt as to the cause of the slump. He reported to the committee set up to examine conditions in the hosiery industry in 1844: 'When ladies garments were worn shorter and the instep seen, they used to take a pride in having a handsome and well-made stocking; but, since the introduction of long petticoats, the moment a lady got a pair of good stockings on, if it was a dusty day they would not be fit to be seen from the dust covering them; that is, if she was walking out, and if it was a wet day they would be all over mud; so that there has been no inducement for any lady to put on a pair of well-fashioned stockings ... '.[45]

To this era, if not before, belong the stockings which are silk up to the lower calf and cotton beyond. The 'Lady in Search of a Good Servant', got drenched in a storm: 'I kept stepping into all kinds of puddles, right up to the cotton tops of my white silk stockings'.[46] This type of stocking survives in quantity; the silk is usually white, pink, or mauve, the cotton top is invariably white with two or more red, pink or blue lines in the welt. These lines, first used in about 1810, probably indicate that the cotton thread was bleached before knitting, and was therefore stronger. There are surviving examples of these silk and cotton stockings dated 1843, 1845 and 1853. Two pairs of stockings dated 1828, in the Victoria and Albert Museum show a variation, machine knitted cotton tops above hand knitted ankles and feet. A similar pair in Nottingham was worn for a wedding in 1843.

Hand knitting from being a utilitarian accomplishment entered the educational curriculum with the *Instructions on Needlework* published in 1832 as a handbook for the National

Schools, and thence into fancy work. From the 1830s to the 1860s numerous small booklets were written by Riego de la Branchardiere, Cornelia Mee, Miss Watts and others, for a growing and skilled market.[47] The fashion magazines, such as *The Lady's Companion* and *The Ladies' Cabinet* started to include knitting patterns. While many of these patterns were for ornamental items, some were for articles of practical clothing, including stockings. A comparatively large number of hand knitted stockings survive from the 1840s onwards; often of rather thick cotton, in plain or fancy knitting, with a short band of ribbing at the top. Some are more delicate, and some are semi-professional work, done in the Irish Schools, for example. Two pairs of white cotton hose of *c* 1840 with blue glass beads knitted in, at Manchester, are thought to be German.[48]

Men's stockings and socks

John Withers Taylor also commented on men's hose: 'The gentlemen...have taken to wearing boots almost universally, and they want nothing under the boot of fine kid. It does not matter to them, perhaps, how the stocking is made, if it will wear as well. All these things have a tendency to drive the manufacture into a lower grade altogether, for an article that is purely invisible in wear'.[49] William Gardiner attributed the decline in the hosiery trade to the fashion for trousers and that, in turn, to an enthusiasm for the navy. '...short knee'd breeches were laid aside for the sailor's trousers. This alteration had a great effect upon the Leicester trade. Stockings were shortened into half hose...This circumstance entirely destroyed the manufacture of those beautiful and curious stockings, which till then, fashion was constantly changing with the utmost variety'.[50] Trousers were already part of working-men's dress and as such adopted by the Jacobins during the French Revolution. They became part of boy's dress in the 1760s and were first worn fashionably by men at Brighton in 1807. Early trousers were short and wide, and stockings would still have been worn with them.

26 Fine white cotton stocking; embroidered openwork at the front of the foot; marked 'A...A' [Allen, Solly & Allen], 1832–5. Length 26½ inches, foot length 8½ inches, 44 stitches per inch, 58 rows per vertical inch

A cross between trousers and breeches – pantaloons – had appeared by the end of the eighteenth century. Made of a stretchable material, frequently wool or silk, on the stocking frame, they clung to the figure to an often indecent extent. In the nineteenth century they were sometimes called 'tights'. They ended between the calf and the ankle and were worn with boots for riding and morning wear, and with shoes for evening dress. George 'Beau' Brummell habitually wore 'a blue coat and waistcoat, black pantaloons which buttoned tight to the ankle, striped silk stockings, and an opera hat' in the evening.[51] Half hose, which are literally half stockings with a welt at the top, could also be worn under pantaloons as the tightness of the pantaloons would keep them in place. In 1816 Captain Gronow adopted the French fashion for evening trousers for a party at Manchester House, London. The Prince Regent initially disapproved, but started to wear them himself shortly afterwards.[52] Trousers continued as an essential part of man's wardrobe but pantaloons started to disappear by the 1830s and were rare by the 1850s.

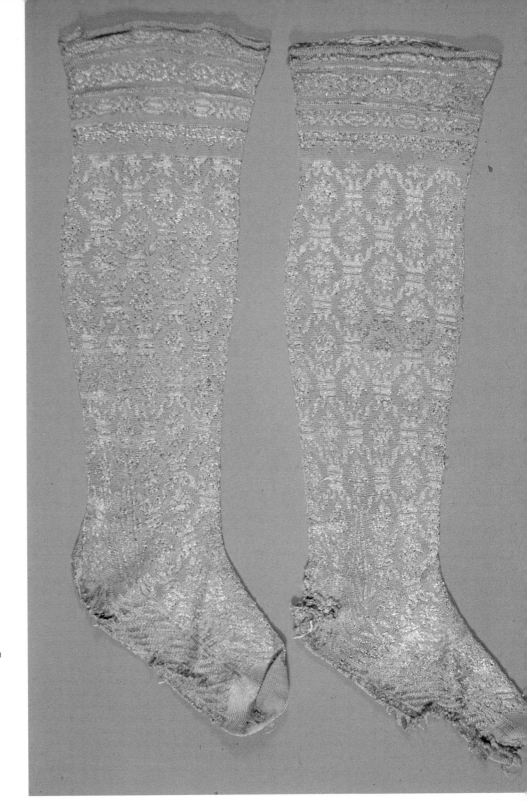

1 Boy's stockings, salmon pink silk with gold and silver thread, hand knitted, late sixteenth or early seventeenth century. The tops are particularly elaborate and were presumably meant to be seen. Length approx. 18½ inches, foot length approx. 8¼ inches.

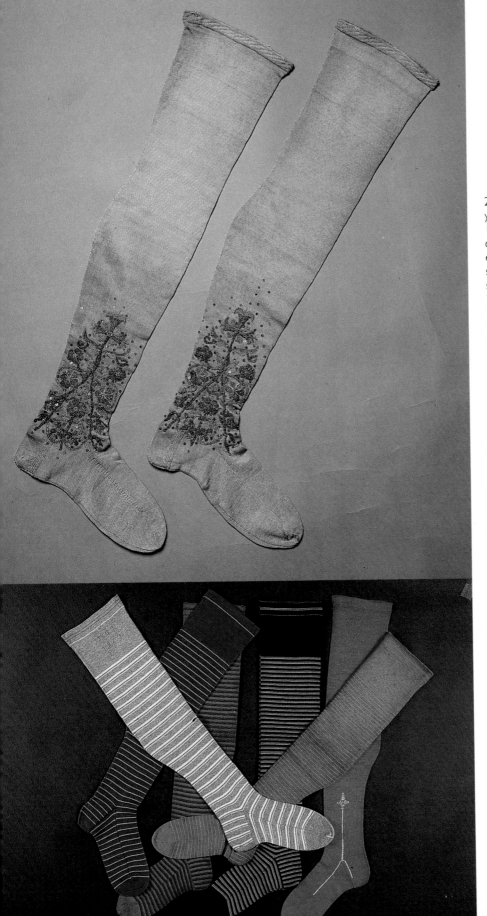

2 Boy's stockings, yellow silk, hand knitted, 1600 – 20; purl stitch clock hidden by embroidery in gold and silver thread and spangles. Length 22 inches, foot length 8½ inches, 25 stitches per inch, 32 rows per vertical inch.

3 (Below) Selection of women's stockings exhibited by Nathanial Corah and Sons of Leicester at the International Exhibition of 1862; all are wool probably dyed with the recently introduced aniline (chemical) dyes developed from coal tar.

4 (Right) Women's silk stockings. From right: black silk with brightly coloured banded fronts, embroidery above c 1870, mark 'B'; space dyed in brown, magenta and yellow, arrowhead clock, labelled inside 'Carrie Samuel, 6, 1881', mark 'M'; black silk, yellow silk, Vandyke top, c 1890, mark 'B'.

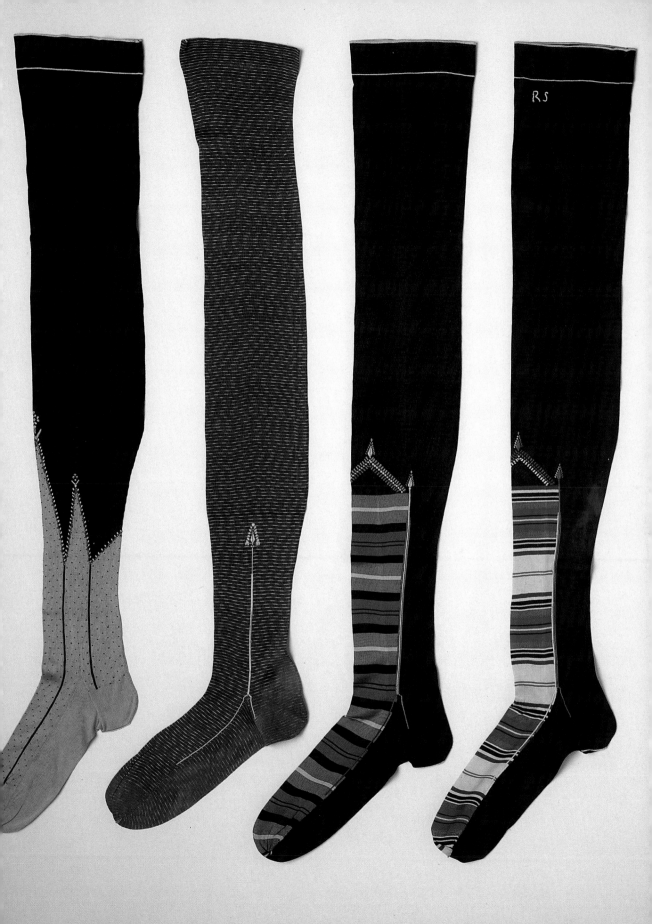

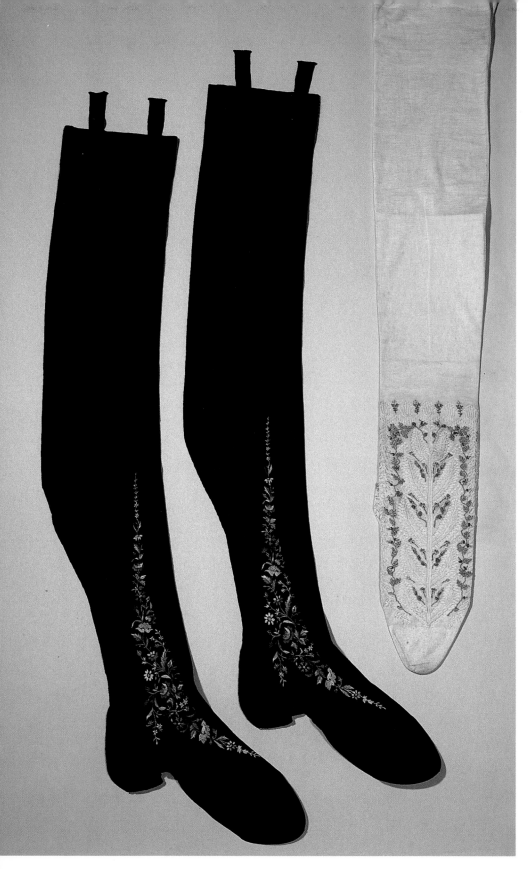

5   (Left) Women's
embroidered stockings.
Right: white lisle, with
embroidery of
oakleaves, acorns,
rosebuds and violets
around elaborate
openwork, 1832 – 5;
mark 'A…A'. Length
27½ inches, foot length
8 inches, 48 stitches per
inch, 54 rows per
vertical inch.
Left: blue silk
embroidered in satin
stitch in coloured silks,
1878 – 84. Length
28 inches, foot length
9 inches, 34 stitches per
inch, 40 rows per
vertical inch.

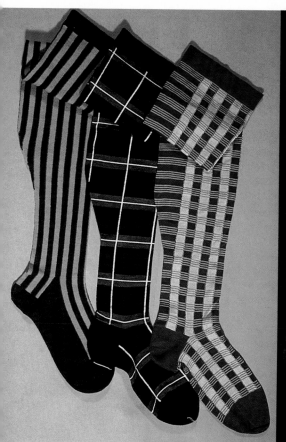

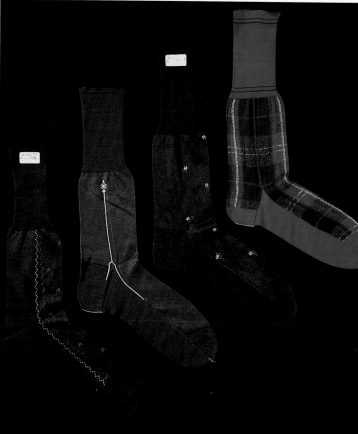

6 (Above left) Women's woollen stockings. Left: late nineteenth century. Length 26½ inches, foot length 9½ inches.
Centre: Black Watch tartan, 1880 – 90. Length 25 inches, foot length 9 inches.
Right: intarsia stripes with bands of yellow lines, c 1900. Length 25 inches, foot length 9 inches.

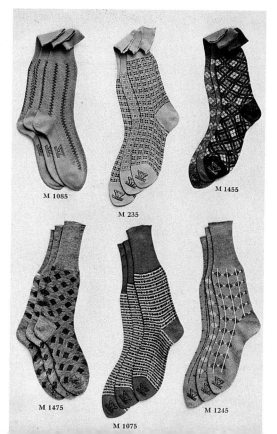

M 1085
M 235
M 1455
M 1475
M 1075
M 1245

7 (Above right) Men's socks, made by I & R Morley Ltd. From right to left: silk, tartan pattern c 1860; silk hand embroidered with flowers c 1904; silk with wool heel, sole, toe and ribbed top, hand embroidered clock, label 'Austin Reed Ltd London' c 1930; silk hand embroidered in silk c 1916.

8 (Left) Men's fancy socks from I & R Morley's catalogue, spring 1930; all cashmere, except the last, and made on the circular machine.

9 *(Opposite)* Pop sox by
Pretty Polly, 1970. Like the
Knee-High stockings of the
1930s Pop Sox (in 13
colours) and Mini-Maxi (in
stocking colours) were
introduced for wear under
longer skirts. In the 1970s
they were also popular
under trousers. Pop sox
and Mini-Maxi were Pretty
Polly trade names.

10 *(Above)* Psychedelic
stockings and tights, French,
1987.

11 *(Left)* Bright yellow
opaque tights by Aristoc,
1990.

12   'Firenze', luxurious tights embroidered in silk and gold thread to retail at £90 a pair; by Fogal of Switzerland, 1992.

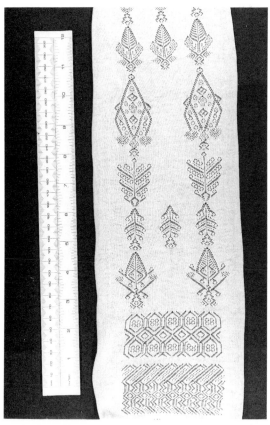

27   Stocking sampler, white cotton Lisle, probably 1830–50; samplers were both an indication of skill on the part of the framework knitter and a library of patterns. Total length 87 inches, width 6 inches

Under trousers half hose needed support. Precisely when they lost the welts and acquired ribbed cuffs to become ankle socks is not clear. There are no ribbed cuffs in the J R Allen Collection. In *An Account of the Machine-wrought Hosiery Trade* by W Felkin, 1845, a number of frames are listed as making 'ribbed tops', probably in fact, the ribbed cuffs to which plain knitted ankle socks would be sewn or grafted. A registered design of 1854 for a pair of child's socks has ribbed cuffs, and a *Punch* cartoon of October 1856 shows ribbed cuffs on a pair of men's banded socks.

Previously the sock had been defined as 'Something to put at the bottom of the feet to keep them warm and dry' (1758)[53] There are two pairs of white cotton 'foot sox' of 1810 and

1815 in the J R Allen Collection, and several pairs of hand knitted woollen ones in Manchester which would fit this description. Similar socks, called 'footlets' were available into the 1930s. In 1815 insoles or socks of plaited horsehair and velvet, lamb's wool or silk shag were worn to keep the feet warm and the damp out. The valetudinarian Mr Merrywinkle put on 'wash-leather socks over his stockings and India rubber shoes over his boots' before venturing into the rain. When he did get wet, his feet were well rubbed by his wife and mother-in-law and clothed in worsted stockings.[54]

Until well into the 1840s men's stockings were visible at the instep above a low-cut shoe, below trousers or pantaloons. Portraits, such as that of John Keats, by Joseph Severn, painted in 1821, or Baron Schwiter, painted by Delacroix in 1826, show plain black or white stockings, but fashion plates, particularly continental ones, show a great variety of ribs and patterns.[55] 'White or striped silk stockings' were specified with a blue or green coat, a coloured neckcloth

28   Fashion plate from The World of Fashion, *January 1832; the stockings worn by the figure on the left have a zigzag pattern and those by the central figure openwork in stripes*

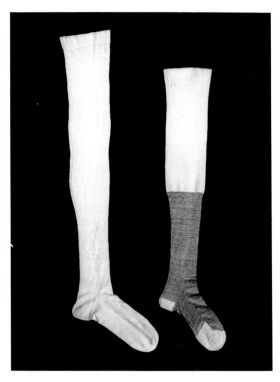

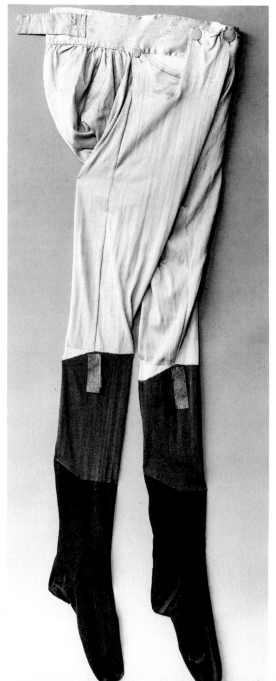

31 **Right:** *John Hookham Frere (1769–1846), by Henry Edridge, 1810–15. Mr Frere is probably wearing white cotton stockings under his trousers*

30 **Below:** *Pantaloons, 1790–1820; framework knitted in yellow (waist to knee), brown and black silk; below the knees they imitate top-boots, even to the linen loops for drawing on; probably worn by one of the sons of Dunbar, 4th Earl of Selkirk; considered more of an individual fancy than a general fashion, though pantaloons with feet attached are known*

29 Left: *cream silk stocking embroidered with crowns and acorns to celebrate Queen Victoria's coronation in 1838; marked '16' inside welt. Length 27½ inches, foot length 9¼ inches. Right: white cotton top; from lower calf space dyed silk in yellow, white, fawn and brown, cotton toe and part of sole; mark, 'A' on welt and small 'l'; 'S J' are the wearer's initials, 1839. Length 24 inches, foot length 8½ inches*

and light coloured trousers strapped under the feet to keep them tight, for morning wear in 1826.[56] The half hose of 1830–50 in the J R Allen Collection show discreet colour and pattern; speckled deep brown bands, or thin coloured bands with drop stitch ribs.

Cotton was worn in the summer or when silk was too expensive. Two of Mr Pickwick's fellow inmates of the Fleet Prison wore white or grey cotton stockings, and Mr Stiggins, the drunken 'deputy shepherd' of a temperance society, had rusty black cotton stockings under his very short trousers (1830).[57] On a fine day Islington clerks 'with large families and small salaries' discarded black gaiters to reveal 'white stockings and cleanly brushed Bluchers [boots].'[58] Four main types of boot were worn during the day: the

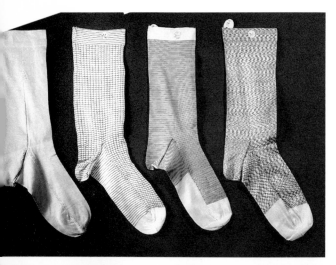

32a   Silk socks, made by Allen & Solly, probably 1830–40, shown at the Great Exhibition in 1851. Left to right, pale lilac with embroidered arrowhead clock, length 11 inches, foot length 9 inches, 38 stitches per inch, 64 rows per vertical inch
White with blue lines, stripes made by taking out a needle every eighth stitch. Length 11¼ inches, foot length 9¼ inches, 40 stitches per inch, 47 rows per vertical inch
White with lines space dyed in blue and black, length 10¼ inches, foot length 9¼ inches, 36 stitches per inch, 44 rows per vertical inch
White, space dyed in black, length 11½ inches, foot length 10 inches, 36 stitches per inch, 42 stitches per vertical inch

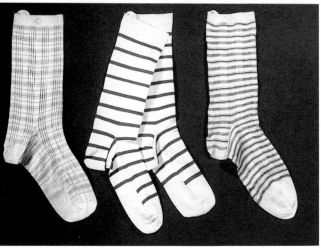

32b   Left to right: white with green bands, stripes made by taking out needles at intervals, length 11¼ inches, foot length 9 inches, 40 stitches per inch, 40 rows per vertical inch
Pink and brown bands, length 12 inches, foot length 9¼ inches, 36 stitches per inch, 44 rows per vertical inch
White with black bands, stripes probably made by using a tuck presser, length 11 inches, foot length 9½ inches, 34 stitches per inch, 60 rows per vertical inch

hessian with a curved top edge to below the knee, the top boot with a deep band of light coloured leather at the top, the Wellington, a short boot popularised by the Duke of Wellington after 1817, and worn only with trousers, and the Blucher, a low boot barely reaching the ankle. In the 1840s to add insult to the injury that the wearing of boots had already given to the hosiery trade, there was an evening Wellington boot with an imitation stocking of black openwork stockinet over the leather.[59]

Gaiters and shoes were worn as an alternative to boots. Mr Pickwick in 1830, wore, with the pantaloons of his youth, dark gaiters over 'speckled silk stockings' which he revealed when intending to dance at a wedding.[60]

Plain or openwork white silk was worn with black or white pantaloons or black trousers for evening wear until the 1830s when black silk became more general. At a Parisian concert in 1826 black coats were worn with white satin waistcoats, white cashmere pantaloons and 'white silk stockings with open clocks', and blue coats with black pantaloons and white or light grey silk stockings.[61] Angelo Cyrus Bantam, a fictional Master of Ceremonies at Bath, wore a blue coat, white waistcoat, black pantaloons and black silk stockings in 1830.[62] In 1839 the Marchioness of Normanby ordered for her husband six pairs of black silk 'net openwork' and six pairs of plain half hose from Barlow & Comyn, of Nottingham.[63] Seeking to impress his host's daughters, Mr Sponge wore for dinner, a velvet collared coat, a pink fancy-fronted shirt, and 'black tights, with broad black and white Cranborne Alley looking stockings (socks rather) and patent leather pumps' (c 1852). John Leech's illustration shows banded socks. Cranborne

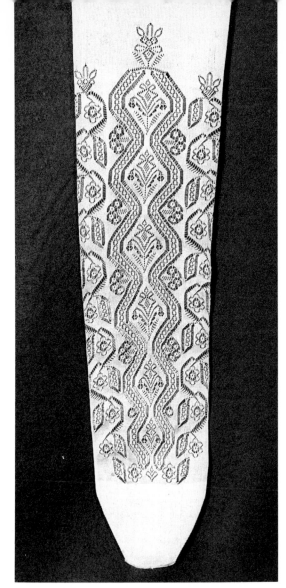

33 *White silk stocking made and shown by I & R Morley at the Great Exhibition 1851. Length 25¼ inches, foot length 9½ inches, 48 stitches per inch, 60 rows per vertical inch*

In 1826 Parisian gentlemen making New Year calls wore 'openwork silk stockings with embroidered clocks' with black cloth coats, violet velvet or silver embroidered moiré waistcoats and black velvet breeches.[66] Some of the larger openwork silk stockings in museum collections may well be men's rather than women's.

Hand or machine knitted white or grey worsted stockings were the most usual wear for countrymen. Occasionally they were brightly coloured. A Tyneside keelman in the early 1800s wore bright blue stockings and a red neckcloth with otherwise dingy clothes.[67] George Borrow noted grey and white lamb's wool stockings during his tour of Wales in 1854, also much hand knitting.[68] Knitting by hand continued as a local industry in the Lake District and the Yorkshire Dales. Water powered mills carded and spun the wool which was then distributed to the knitters. In some areas, Swaledale for instance, the yarn was thick 'bump', knitted into what children called 'elephant stockings' from their hugeness, and shrunk to the correct size.[69] The trade was considerable. In the 1820s the produce of Swaledale and Wensleydale was worth £40,000. Most of it was exported. Knitting schools were set up in various areas, sometimes as a means of Poor Relief, as at Kendal in 1800, or to teach a means of livelihood. One such was founded in Nottingham in 1799 under the patronage of Lady Middleton. Two mistresses taught spinning and knitting to a total of ninety-eight girls in 1800.[70]

The Great Exhibition, 1851

From the mid nineteenth century, the series of international exhibitions, which began with the Great Exhibition held in London in 1851, offered an excellent showcase for hosiery, and all the main firms exhibited. The *Report of the Jury* in 1851 commended English hosiery, finding the bleach and finish of Nottingham cotton hosiery unequalled, and the range, colour and shape of Leicester's hosiery surprisingly diversified. France was complimented on her silk stockings, particularly the 'beautifully designed and executed chevening'. German cotton hosiery

Alley in London was notorious for cheap, flashy clothing.[64]

For balls and other very formal occasions breeches and stockings were still correct dress. Generally white stockings, plain, embroidered or openwork were worn with white breeches, black, usually with an embroidered clock, with black breeches. At a levée in 1812 or 1813 William Gardiner saw the Prince Regent ablaze with diamonds, in white casimir breeches and 'lace silk stockings, gold buckles on the shoes, finishing the handsomest leg and foot I ever beheld'.[65]

made in Saxony was however not considered equal to the English. Brief entries in the official catalogues probably conceal extensive displays as each firm would try to show the complete range of its wares. I & R Morley (having one of the longer descriptions in 1851) exhibited white cotton and Lisle thread stockings, silk stockings with cotton tops and lace openwork, men's cotton half hose, some with spun silk double feet ('curious'), with fancy merino feet or real beaver feet ('superior'). Pope & Plante, of London, also showed 'beaver fur stockings'. Examples of their half hose with openwork mottoes 'Peace and Prosperity', and 'By Industry We thrive' are in the Victoria and Albert Museum.[71] Nottingham has the collection exhibited by Allen & Solly, and some of Morley's silk stockings. Both Leicester and Manchester have woollen stockings, dated in the knitting, shown by N Corah & Sons, of Leicester at the International Exhibition in 1862. Corah also exhibited in 1851. Various Scottish firms including Alexander Hadden & Sons, of Aberdeen, and Kaye, Findlay & Co of Langholm and Glasgow, showed machine knitted woollen hosiery. At least two firms showed Shetland knitting: ladies' brown and white stockings, natural coloured socks, white knee caps and brown leggings. William Whitehead & Son, Edinburgh, exhibited worsted tartan hose ('containing 1,300 diamonds') made on a 32 gauge frame, and silk tartan hose made on a 42 gauge frame. Ward, Sturt, Sharp & Ward, of Belper and London showed a range of cotton and Lisle thread hose made on 24 to 70 gauge frames, the latter being the finest gauge then possible.

J B & W Nevill & Co, London, exhibited men's striped cotton half hose, white linen thread hose and, intriguingly, 'imitation silk thread hose'. The linen thread hose were made from Irish flax, but Ireland's most famous contribution to hosiery at this period were the cotton products of Balbriggan, north of Dublin. Smyth & Co of Balbriggan founded in the late eighteenth century, made men's and women's hose from soft, silky Orleans or Sea Island cotton.[72] Six or eight threads were used together instead of the two or three in England. Balbriggan became a

34 White cotton stocking with openwork decoration, from a trousseau of 1859; marked on welt '60' and three holes; twisted back seam. length 24 inches, foot length 10 inches, 36 stitches per inch, 44 rows per vertical inch

generic term for fine cotton hosiery, to the extent that in 1882 steps were taken to prevent the name being used on spurious or inferior fabric. In the late nineteenth century Balbriggan's products were chiefly of wool. Smyth & Co did not exhibit in 1851 but Balbriggan hosiery, mainly lace stockings and socks (some of seven threads with nine threads in heels and feet) were shown by four other firms, including I & R Morley.

Among the technical developments in 1851 was a frame which could make 'in a week as many frame-work sacks as can be cut and sewn up into seventy-five to one hundred dozens of small women's hose.'[73] Each dozen weighed fourteen ounces and was offered at 2s 2d per dozen, three and a half ounces lighter in weight and 1s 5d cheaper in price than 'cut-up' stockings made on the wide frame. This was the shape of things to come.

1860–1920

Developments in machinery

Writing in 1838 William Gardiner could see the effect that the power driven loom had had on the expansion of the cotton weaving industry and the lack of power was having on the hosiery industry. 'The Stocking Trade at Leicester has never risen to a degree of importance owing to the slow operation of weaving by hand (i.e. by hand operated machines). Hose can be wrought equally cheap in Scotland or Germany'.[1] In 1844 Felkin saw the problem more in terms of mechanics: 'Such is the speed of the hands and the difficulty of putting in fashion by power wrought frames, that the superseding by the latter of the former seems to be very unlikely and remote'.[2] Within twenty years, however, that breakthrough had been achieved.

The two main mechanical difficulties were, firstly, adapting a linear operation to rotary power, such as the wheel driven by hand, water or steam, and secondly achieving the shaping or fashioning of the hose automatically. The first, it seems, had already been achieved by 1838, when Luke Barton patented a wide frame in which the stitches were shifted automatically thus realising the second.[3] Jules-Nicholas Poivret's machine of *c* 1840 and A Simon's of 1856 (both in the Musée de la Bonneterie at Troyes) were largely superseded by Arthur Paget's machines, patented in 1857, 1859 and 1860.[4] Chiefly by using a special type of thread carrier, Paget's machines were able to fashion the stocking without needing to stop or slow down. Though efficient they were difficult to set up and maintain; and were eclipsed by William Cotton's machine, patented in 1863.[5] Cotton's machine, also made at Loughborough like Paget's, not only fashioned the stocking, but also made more

than one at the same time, with needles that operated vertically rather than horizontally. With the addition of steam power Cotton's machines could produce hose cheaply and in quantity.

There was, however, an alternative to the rotary operated frame; the circular machine, in which the needles were placed in a ring. The first inventions seem to have been made in France by Decroix in 1798, Aubert in 1803 and Leroy in 1808, probably for making tubular caps.[6] In 1816 Marc Brunel patented 'Le Tricoteur' a circular machine small enough to be clamped to a lady's work table, but did not develop it further. Peter Clausen of Brussels improved it in the 1840s, but on trying to sell the machine in England encountered some opposition. Although admired for its speed, it could only make a tube which had to be cut and sewn into stockings. By 1845 the hosiery industry was just beginning to crawl out of a recession and 'cut ups' were seen as an unacceptable cheapening of the product. Matthew Townsend patented a hinged or 'tumbler' needle in 1849, thus replacing one of the few parts of Lee's machine which remained in the circular one.[7] Townsend took his invention to America where there was already a considerable hosiery industry chiefly in Philadelphia.

American and English inventions often seem to occur within a few years of each other.[8] In 1831 Egbert Egberts and Timothy Baily adapted a stocking frame to work by rotary motion and attached it to a water wheel in 1832. Joseph Button, previously from Leicester, adapted a machine for making children's hosiery to steam power in 1838 and in 1839 Richard Walker of Portsmouth, New Hampshire, patented a 'rotary power stocking loom'. Great interest was shown in the circular machine. In 1855 Jonas B and Walter Aiken patented a single cone circular machine and in 1858 double cone for rib knitting. Both used a 'latch' needle patented by James Hibberd in 1850, which was similar to Townsend's tumbler needle. (Hine, Mundella and Thomas Thompson patented improvements to the circular ribbing machine in 1853.) An American, William Clark Grist, took out an English patent in 1858 for a circular machine with up to eight feeders, enabling coloured banding to be more easily made, and, incidentally, a much more evenly knitted fabric. His machine worked at a rate of 350 rows a minute, and could produce sufficient fabric to make a hundred and fifty dozen pairs of women's stockings a week. During the American Civil War, to keep up with increased demand, stockings were made as tubes to which separately made heels and toes were added.[9] By 1870 socks were being made automatically and continuously on the circular machine needing only to be separated and have the heel and toe joined by hand. Within a few years a fully automatic machine could make socks with the toe and heels closed.[10] Much larger circular machines made underwear and sports garments.

The industrial circular machine had an offshoot in the hand operated domestic machine. The first of these domestic machines was apparently 'The Lamb', introduced before 1869, and according to one recommendation, over 'four hundred pairs of socks and stockings were made up by a private soldier at a cost of three farthings less per pair than the Government price'.[11] A child of twelve could knit his own socks on a 'Climax' Knitting Machine; and the 'Crane' and the 'Little Rapid' both had their advocates.[12] In 1870 Henry J Griswold invented a hand operated knitting machine, and in 1879 patented a circular machine in which the cylinder remained stationary while the cam-box moved round it.[13] His seems the most popular machine on a semi-industrial basis but, later on in the century, other machines made by the firms of Higham and Harrison of Manchester, and James Foster of Preston were advertised in magazines, and sometimes recommended by the same periodicals

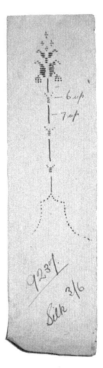

35 *An example of a chevening pattern, c 1912, for C Coggan & Co Ltd, Hosiery Manufacturers, Nottingham*

to young women wishing to earn money working at home. Many of these machines had another lease of life during the depression of the 1930s. They were used chiefly for making men's and children's socks.

The application of steam power to the rotary and circular machines and in particular to Cotton's machine encouraged the larger manufacturer to build or move into factories. Hine and Mundella were the first in Nottingham, and their factory was described as 'one of the most handsome buildings in the town' and 'the best specimen of the new class of factory yet erected'.[14] Ward, Strutt, Sharp & Ward had thirty ordinary frames, thirty-six circular machines and six or eight 'very wide ones that go by steam power' in their factory at Belper by 1854.[15] The circular machines had created a demand for better quality, fashioned hose. Morley's built their first factory in Manvers Road, Nottingham in 1866, and Corah of Leicester their St Margaret Works in 1865, but Allen, Solly & Co's factory was not built until 1888, relatively late.[16]

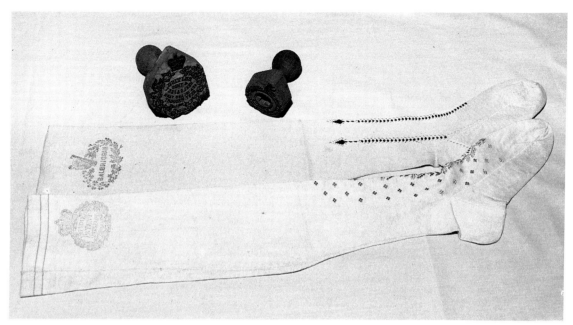

36 Carved wooden stamps, both with holes for exchangeable inserts, c 1865, used by Alexander Ogden & Co, Denby, Derbyshire; stocking of cream cotton, with black and white chevening, stamped 'Balbriggan', and stocking of white cotton with blue chevening, stamped 'Improved Patent 2 threads, 4 thds heels & feet'; both made by Ward, Sturt & Sharp, Belper, 1870–90

In the large firms most of the knitting and finishing was done in the factory, but outworkers were employed to do the seaming and chevening. At the end of the nineteenth century Morley employed 450 makers-up and 500 cheveners in and around Nottingham.[17] Finishing included 'scouring' (for cotton hose) in soap and water with the addition of ammonia or soda; or 'milling' (for merino hose) in a soap lather with friction to bring the wool to the surface; spin-drying, dyeing, 'trimming' or stretching on a stocking shaped board, and drying in a steam press. Cotton goods were pressed between sheets of cardboard to impart a gloss, and merino and woollen hose were passed through wire or teazle brushes to raise the nap, before being pressed. After a final inspection the hose was often stamped with the firm's name and indication of the fibre content 'Improved Merino' or 'Balbriggan' for example, in ink or a concoction of starch and launderer's blue, which washed out. Other

marks, the initial(s) of the firm and holes to indicate size (one for small, two for medium, three for large) had already been put in by hand in the knitting. Hose and half-hose were packed in boxes of a dozen or half-dozen.

Firms could be huge. Probably the largest in the 1890s was I & R Morley with ten factories and warehouses in London, Nottingham and Leicester, Heanor in Derbyshire, Sutton-in-Ashfield, Nottinghamshire and Loughborough, Leicestershire, and a workforce, excluding outworkers, of 4,664. But by this time, knitted underwear and sports garments were being produced as well as socks and stockings.

The specialist framework knitter

From the 1860s the great bulk of hosiery production came from the large factories, but framework knitting by craftsmen in their homes, or in small complexes, continued into the present century. In 1948, for instance, Allen, Solly & Co employed four framework knitters in a small factory in Calverton.[18] Much of what they did was high quality work for special orders. John Meakin (1816–1898) a frameworker employed by Morley in Derby, made stockings for Queen Victoria from before her Accession in 1837 until his death.[19] These stockings are marked inside the welt with a small 'S' for Swears and Wells, who placed the order, and Meakin's own initials 'JM'. An 'M' for Morley usually appears below the welt. In 1898 the Queen and he exchanged photographs and she also possessed a photograph of Ann Birkin (also born in 1816) of Ruddington, who had embroidered the Queen's stockings for sixty years.[20] In recent years a framework knitters' complex has been restored at Ruddington. Although wide frames are once again in use they make only shawls; socks and stockings are made on Griswold circular machines.

Quantities and colours of women's stockings

In the early 1870s Felkin noted a decline in the numbers of knitters on silk frames from 1,666 in the East Midland counties in 1844 to 135 in 1866.[21] This he blamed on changes of fashion and the weighting of thin silks with dyes to make them appear to be of better quality, but it might have been the result of the first enthusiasm for cheap factory made goods. Certainly from the 1860s stockings (and men's socks) in individual wardrobes were counted in dozens rather than singly. For the trousseau of an upper middle class bride in 1872 twelve pairs of cotton stockings, twelve pairs of spun silk and six pairs of silk stockings were recommended.[22] An Irish woman who married in 1878 had a dozen pairs of Balbriggan and half-a-dozen pairs of woollen stockings in her trousseau.[23] A similar amount, one dozen pairs of thread hose, and half-a-dozen pairs of either merino or spun silk were suggested for a girl in middle class society in 1883.[24] An inexpensive trousseau in 1890 contained four pairs of black spun silk, four pairs of Lisle and eight pairs of black cashmere stockings. The spun silk and cashmere hose cost 2s 6d a pair, the Lisle 1s 11d.[25] One Parisian elegante who claimed to have 'forty-two dozen pairs of silk stockings, striped, embroidered, plain, openworked, and spangled with gold and silver threads' in 1875 was surely exceptional.[26]

She might, of course have been taking literally

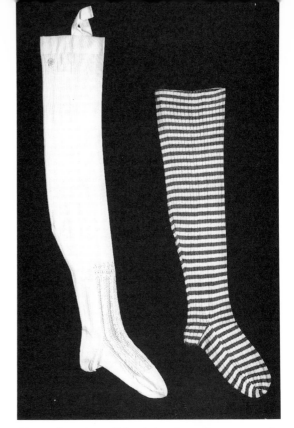

37   Right: *white silk banded with purple, stripes made by taking out needles at intervals, c 1865*
Left: *cream silk, with embroidered openwork at front, worn by Princess Louise of Prussia for her marriage to Arthur, Duke of Connaught, third son of Queen Victoria, in 1879*

fashion's dictum that stockings had to match the dress in colour. The Empress Eugenie, the elegant wife of the Emperor Napoleon III of France, had started this particular trend in the early 1860s.[27] According to the fashion magazines, which were springing up to cater for a middle and even working class clientele, the match had to be exact. 'Nothing can be more revolting to taste and unpleasant to the eyes than different shades of colour placed in close proximity and not matching well together... the most striking contrasts of colour would look infinitely better than those would-be similar and ill-matched tints'.[28] This was applicable to stockings for, during the 1860s, the skirt was looped up onto the artificial crinoline for walking. This fashion, too, was attributed to the Empress Eugenie at the coastal resort of Trouville. The artificial crinoline replaced heavy, bulky, starched petticoats from 1856 to 1866. Made of watch-spring steel, its buoyancy was a gift to cartoonists and hosiers, as the swing of it could reveal the stockings to a startling extent. Stockings banded in black and a colour to match the petticoat were particularly popular.[29] Even after the crinoline had metamorphosed into the bustle at the end of the decade, and drapery and trains had displaced short skirts, stockings still had to match the dress. Blue spun silk stockings spotted with white were worn with a 'peasant's blue' cambric dress with large white spots during summers in the early 1870s.[30] Richly embroidered coloured silk and the cheaper thread stockings to match the dress were worn throughout the 1870s. White stockings were no longer fashionable unless, of course, the dress was white. In 1875 some stockings matched the slippers, for indoor wear: 'Slippers of pearl grey rep, embroidered with rosebuds, with grey stockings, also embroidered with the same'.[31] *Cassell's Family Magazine* commented in 1878 'The suit of dittoes that men affected in days gone by was never carried out so thoroughly as is observable in ladies' summer fashions'.[32] The bonnet or hat, the boots or shoes, and the parasol were to be made of the same material as the dress with gloves, stockings and handbag to match. But such a fashion was costly, and therein lay its exclusiveness. From 1880 black appeared as an alternative particularly for day dress, and in the mid 1880s both shoes and stockings matched the dress: 'White shoes and stockings are worn with white dresses in the evening; black shoes with black; bronze shoes with brown dresses; otherwise the colour of both the shoes and stockings match the dress!'.[33] If this was impossible then for most of the 1880s and 1890s shoes and stockings alone had to match, black with black, bronze or brown with bronze (in the 1880s) or tan with tan or brown from 1888. Exceptionally in 1884 black stockings were worn with black dresses and scarlet leather shoes.[34] In the early 1890s the rule abated: stockings could match the dress exactly or recall the colour of trimming or accessory: 'Thus with a dress of dark navy-blue with a red pattern, the stockings are identically alike; with a coffee-coloured dress, trimmed with blue, they are coffee-coloured, embroidered with blue silk

spots, and so on'.[35] But with an evening dress of mauve crepe, mauve silk stockings with an openwork pattern, embroidered in violet, were worn. By 1895 stockings had to match the dress again, and the fashion even extended to golfing and cycling costume. Up to World War I the rule remained more or less in force. The couturiere 'Lucile' described approvingly an all brown dance frock of satin with a chiffon overtunic, and shoes, stockings and hat ribbons to match in June 1914.[36] Throughout much of this period skirts were at least floor length, becoming an inch or two shorter in the late 1870s and early 1880s, and an inch or two longer around 1900. When skirts for sporting activities were ankle length in the 1890s, leather or cloth gaiters were usually worn. For cycling in the mid 1890s stockinet gaiters were sometimes preferred; a revival of the 'elastic' gaiter of 1843.[37]

Colours varied considerably in this period. In the early 1860s they were sharp and bright; magenta and solferino, the new aniline dyes, developed from coal-tar, and named after battles in the Italian war of unification were particularly popular. Crinoline petticoats in these colours matching stockings banded in black were seen, also scarlet with scarlet. Other bright colours – blues, greens, mauves – followed. Light shades of these colours were fashionable in the early 1870s being replaced in 1873 by colours that were 'more sickly than ever; we have consumptive green, fainting grey and dead turquoise' and a serpent green 'I can only liken to green-pea soup'.[38] 'Miserable tints of drab, brown, black, enlivened only by white or filleul, making their wearers look like lichened boles of trees' were succeeded by rainbow colours in August 1877.[39] In December the fashionable colours were olive green, moss green, plum, maroon, grey and blue, and for the smart Parisian, black. Many colours of the 1880s are dark in tone; dark blue was popular for stockings, with coloured clocks in 1881. Black enlivened by a bright colour was fashionable in the 1890s, until, towards the turn of the century pastel shades were preferred. Colours were floral by 1914; 'the pale green of a lily leaf combined with white is a delicious colour scheme for a debutante, and so are, of course, the faint blush pinks of the wild rose, the blues of myosotis and the periwinkle, and the pale lavender of the Parma violet'.[40] Barbaric colours and colour schemes, inspired by Leon Bakst's designs for Diaghilev's ballets *Cleopatra* (1909) and *Scheherezade* (1910), were also in evidence. Towards the end of and just after World War I brightly coloured hose were worn by those with artistic leanings. In *Women in Love* by D H Lawrence (written between 1913 and 1919)[41] Gudrun wears emerald green stockings with a blue and green dress, dark green stockings with a dark brown and green striped coat, trimmed with black and orange, bright rose stockings with a pale yellow knitted jacket, and in the Alps, royal blue and scarlet stockings. She gives thick French silk stockings, in vermilion, cornflower blue and grey, to her sister, Ursula, who also likes colourful contrasts, canary coloured stockings with an orange knitted coat, for instance. This is the last flowering of colourful stockings before the beiges and browns of the 1920s.

In every decade to 1900 one colour continually reappears: red. As scarlet in the early 1860s, as red in 1878 on parasols, bonnets, sashes, stockings and neutral coloured costumes, as dark red in 1879, as ruby, strawberry, and brick reds in 1883, as jerseys and stockings, particularly with white in 1887 and 1888, as stockings decorated with swallows in 1887 or with morocco shoes in 1897, and, triumphantly, as scarlet stockings with red shoes in 1899. Yet, 'with the exception of scarlet we would recommend a faithful adherence to black and bronze'.[42]

Black and white

By 1900 black stockings were so common that nineteen out of every twenty pairs made were black.[43] This was not the result of the Victorian penchant for mourning but the results of larger, dirtier towns, the wearing of leather rather than fabric footwear, and better dyes. Black was always unreliable as a colour, apt to go green or brown if not properly cared for. *The Queen*, *The Girl's Own Paper*, and other magazines, frequently contain recipes for the correct wash-

ing of black, or recommend certain hosiers' products as fast dyed. William Elliot of Nottingham had developed a fast black dye for silk in the mid eighteenth century, probably from logwood and chrome, thereby creating another incentive for framework knitters to quit London for the provinces.[44] Cotton and wool were dyed with a conventional dye, again probably of logwood and a mordant, until 1887 when Morley used aniline salts and other chemicals, oxidised by steam to create their famous 'Sanitary dye' for cotton; sanitary in that it did not stain the feet.[45] Other firms followed suit. A E Hawley & Co Ltd, the Sketchley Dye Works, Hinckley, Leicestershire, advertised their hygenic dye 'warranted stainless and acid proof' in 1919.[46] The problem with fastness was not entirely solved however. *The Girl's Own Paper* in 1897 warned against the poor dye of German black thread stockings.[47]

Black stockings were plain or adorned in various ways; with embroidered black or coloured clocks in 1877 and 1882, or with embroidered fronts in the early 1880s, spotted to match the dress in 1885, ribbed in the late 1880s, embroidered to match the dress in 1889, vertically striped with red, white or gold in 1890, or openworked for 1893. Two 'Aesthetic' sisters wore black Irish thread stockings embroidered in old gold with saffron India muslin and old gold silk dresses to a party in 1882.[48] From the late 1890s black stockings were often embroidered with coloured silk flowers up the fronts to upper calf level, or with little posies on the instep in 1907. Coarse black stockings were worn by many working women. The Cullercoats fishwives on Tyneside wore black for every day and coloured for best.[49] Black wool stockings were generally worn for any kind of athletic activity from the 1890s into the 1920s, often with the black or navy blue serge gymslip introduced in 1885.[50] Black hose were even worn for swimming. Consuelo Vanderbilt remembered wearing black silk stockings with a blue alpaca bathing dress in the 1890s, but in Britain black wool was more common, and colours after 1910.[51] Black was general wear for children too, even with white broderie anglaise dresses. As

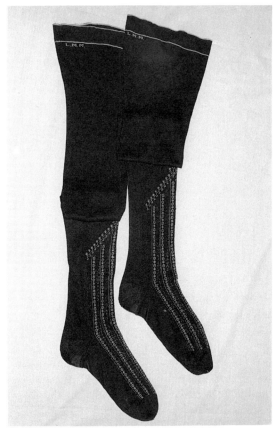

38 Black silk stockings, openwork fronts with white silk embroidery; made by B Walton of Sutton-in-Ashfield for the trousseau of Laura Marianne Morley (née Birch) who married S Hope Morley in 1884; the chevening was done by Mrs Cotton of Derby and the initials by Miss Emma Shacklock, senior hosemender at I & R Morley, Fletcher Gate, Nottingham; mark 'M'

Loelia, Duchess of Westminster explains, 'white stockings were thought to be common'.[52]

From being ubiquitous up to the mid nineteenth century white went into a decline, partly because it was difficult to keep it unsoiled even for half-a-day in the increasingly dirty towns. Openworked white hose were worn with low-cut, sandalled leather shoes in the late 1860s and 1870s, (The Englishwoman's Domestic Magazine had a three year long correspondence on the delights of this style), white, pale salmon pink, or grey were preferred as they showed up the black ribbon of the sandal better. In 1874 The Young Ladies' Journal commented that

Frenchwomen considered English bright striped stockings unladylike and wore fine white stockings exclusively.[53] This was one Parisian fashion not popular across the Channel. Attempts were made to revive the white stocking in 1888 and 1889, and as Lisle thread with coloured floral designs alternating with openwork in 1882, but in general English fashion writers rejoiced in its absence. In 1893 Paris decreed that only white stockings were admissible for evening but by 1897 'one realises that their day is over' except openworked for wear with white dresses and shoes at the seaside.[54] Even then black with the white dress was permissible and, in fact, more usual. The charm of the white stocking which The Lady's Realm extolled in 1915, was in reality the charm of 'delicate shades of fawn, cream and flesh pink' worn with black shoes.[55]

Shoe fashions influence hosiery

In the early 1860s shoes were worn indoors and boots for outside. Fabric, silk satins, or wool, over kid, or kid itself in various colours harmonised with the dress, and stockings conformed. In 1862 house shoes with heels of blue, violet, green or scarlet leather were worn with silk or cotton stockings with embroidered spots matching the leather.[56] In the next decade plain boots in wool satin matching the dress in colour or in black silk satin were preferred to the barette boot with its openwork straps up the front revealing a glimpse of the stocking beneath. Boots gave rise to stockings imitating a side buttoning boot in 1880, or, more prosaically, stockings with silk uppers and cotton or wool feet and ankles.[57]

Evening shoes to beyond the end of the century tended to be more or less low-cut court shoes, without straps, often of satin and in white. There were exceptions. In 1889 The Lady's Pictorial noticed a pair of Parisian evening boots with leather vamps and openwork black silk uppers which laced at the sides.[58] Beneath them coloured socks would be worn. Leicestershire Museums have a pair of black silk stockings with openwork fronts and a panel of red stockinet grafted in behind, which might belong to this era.[59] For day wear the shoe became as important

HOSIERY DEPARTMENT.

Ladies' Black Lisle Thread Hose.

Plain ...	1/11½	2/-	2/11	3/6	3/11	4/6	4/11 per pair.
Silk Clox ...		2/6	2/11	3/6	4/3	4/11 to 6/3	"
Lace Ankles	1/11½	2/6	2/11	3/6	3/11	4/11 " 7/11	"
All Lace... ...	1/11½	2/6	2/11	3/11	4/6	5/6	"
Wide Ribbed ...	...	...	...		3/11	4/6	"

Ladies' Fast Black Cotton Hose.

Silk Clox ...	1/11½	2/6	2/11	3/6	3/11	4/6	5/6 per pair.
Wide Ribbed ...		3/3	3/6	4/3	4/11	5/3	6/3 "

Ladies' Black Summer Cashmere Hose.

Plain ...	1/11½	2/6	2/11	3/3	3/6	3/11	4/6 per pair.
Silk Clox ...		2/11	3/3	3/9	4/6	4/11	6/3 "
Ribbed ...		2/6	3/3	3/9	3/11	4/11	7/3 "
Lace Ankles ...	...	1/11½	2/6	2/11	3/9	4/6	"

Ladies' Black Spun Silk Hose.

Plain	2/9	3/9	4/11	5/6	6/6 to 10/9 per pair.
Lace Ankles ...	3/6	5/9	6/9	Ribbed 6/11 9/6	"

Ladies' Black Pure Silk Hose.

Silk Clox ...	5/11	7/11	10/3	11/9	14/6 to 18/6 per pair.
Lace Ankles ...	6/11	8/11	10/9	12/6	14/6 " 22/6	"
Ribbed	...	...	...		17/9	19/6 "

Ladies' White and Colored Silk Hose.

Plain ...	...	...	...	...	5/11	11/6 per pair.
Lace Ankles	...	...	...	7/6	12/6	15/9 "

Ladies' Openwork Lisle Thread Hose. 1/11 per pair. In every shade

Ladies' Fine Ribbed Silk and Lisle Hose. Black with Colored Shot Effects, 4/6 per pair.

Ladies' All Lace Lisle Thread Hose. 1/11½ 2/11 3/11 per pair. In Black or Tan

Ladies' Fine Ribbed Shot Hose.

Silk and Lisle ...	...	...	...	...	4/6 per pair.
Fine Silk and Cashmere	...	...	...	4/9	"
Pure Spun Silk ...	...	...	...	...	11/6	"
Pure Silk ...	...	...	...	...	22/6	"

Ladies' Colored Spun Silk Hose.

Plain ...	...	...	...	3/6	4/11 per pair.
Lace Ankles	...	...	...	3/6	7/3 "

Ladies' Black Pure Silk Hose.

Embroidered Fronts ...	...	9/11	11/9	16/9 per pair.
Lace Inserted Fronts ...	...	16/9	23/6	33/6 "

Ladies' Tan Lisle Thread Hose.

Lace Ankles ...	...	...	...1/11	2/9	3/9 per pair.
Silk Clox ...	...	...	...	2/9	3/3	"
Cashmere, Plain	2/11	3/11	4/6	Ribbed 3/3	3/11	"
Cotton, Plain	...	...	2/6	3/6	Ribbed 3/6	"

Ladies' White Lisle Thread Hose.

Plain ...	...	...	...1/11½	2/6	2/11	3/6 per pair.
Lace Ankles	...	...	...1/11	2/6	2/11	3/9 "
All Lace ..	...	...	...1/11½	2/6	2/11	3/11 "

Ladies' Black Lisle Thread Hose.

Lace and Embroidered Silk Fronts	2/11	3/6	3/11	4/11

A detailed Catalogue of Ladies' and Children's Hosiery sent post free on application.

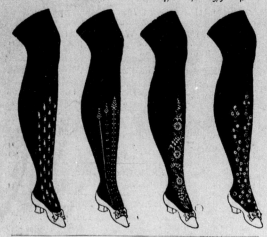

Ladies' Fast Black Hose.

Hand Embroidered Silk Fronts, in great variety, Lisle Thread, Cotton and Summer Cashmere.

2/6 2/11 3/3 3/6 3/11 4/6 4/11 5/6 5/11 per pair.

Also in Spun Silk ... ... 4/6 5/6 6/11 7/6 "

DICKINS & JONES, Ltd., REGENT STREET, LONDON.

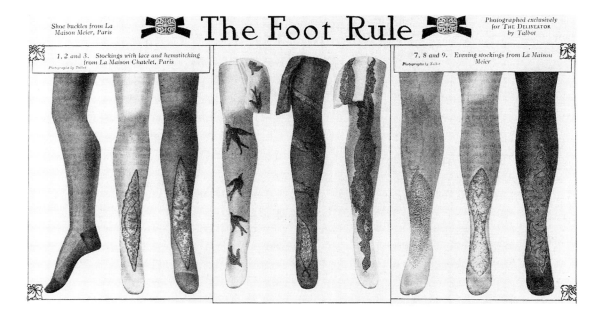

Shoe buckles from La Maison Meier, Paris

The Foot Rule

Photographed exclusively for THE DELINEATOR by Talbot

1, 2 and 3. Stockings with lace and hemstitching from La Maison Chatelet, Paris
Photographs by Talbot

7, 8 and 9. Evening stockings from La Maison Meier
Photographs by Talbot

as the boot. None of the various styles, the Oxford in 1878, the buttoned shoe a decade later, the Puritan, Cromwell and pilgrim shoes from 1887 had much effect on stocking styles. In 1899 the trellis shoe with numerous jet or steel beaded straps allowed a glimpse of openwork stocking. All these shoes, often in brown or black leather offered a contrast to decorative stockings.

Openwork and lace stockings

Openwork stockings were relatively cheap. In 1887 and 1888 D H Evans, a London store, offered 'Lace lisle fashioned, in light shades at 1s 6½d a pair' and Dickins & Jones, another London store, in black Lisle from 1s 11½d to 7s 11d, and in pure silk from 6s 11d to 22s 6d in 1902. These had lace ankles, the openwork often in vertical stripes with stylised trees at the top, and would have been made by Jacquard attachments. In the late 1880s and 1890s there were a number of patents adapting the Jacquard to various knitting machines. The most expensive openwork stockings had insertions of hand

39   Left: From a Dickins & Jones catalogue c 1902. The openwork and all lace Lisle thread hose seem to have been particularly popular.

40   Examples of stockings with lace inserts, from The Delineator, July 1914

made lace and sold at more than £5 5s a pair.[60] Ovals and fern-like designs were noted in 1879, fronts and medallions of lace (unspecified) with embroidered edges in 1880, lace at the sides in 1899. Chantilly, a black silk bobbin lace or it's machine made imitations was used from 1900, with Alencon, Point de France and Valenciennes laces in 1911.[61] *The Delineator* in July 1914 illustrated stockings with lace insertions from the Paris houses of Chatelet and Meier. Stockings from Gastineau have lace swallows or snakes entwining up them, an echo of the silver sequinned snake exhibited at the Paris Exhibition in 1900,[62] or the green sequinned snakes, birds, and butterflies mentioned in *Home Fashions* in May 1914. On the eve of World War I skirts were extremely narrow, often draped at the hips and overlapped in front to show the feet. The new dances of the period, the turkey-trot, the Boston glide and, above all, the tango, showed off these beautiful stockings to perfection. There was even a revival of the sandalled shoe, now called the cothurne. In 1912 the couturier Poiret had introduced a skirt slit up the side and a 'Directoire' silk stocking, transparent enough to show the skin. *The Ladies' Field* commented: 'We shall, if this fashion becomes at all popular, frequently see sights more amusing than beautiful'.[63]

Silk and cotton

Pure silk stockings were still the most coveted and many aristocratic girls did not have their first pair until they were 'out'. Slightly cheaper were spun silk, made from waste silk of broken cocoons. Morleys had exhibited spun silk shirts, children's gloves and men's socks with spun silk feet at the Great Exhibition in 1851, but in the 1870s a new method of manufacturing it must have been developed for in 1879 spun silk hosiery is described as 'only very recently become a luxury within the reach of the middle classes'.[64] Mr C L Lester of Yorkshire is credited, in 1889, with being 'the founder of an entirely new branch of the silk trade, ie that of spun silk'.[65] Silk stockings were carefully washed by hand in cool water and fine soap. When damaged they could be refooted by Barlow & Comyn, Long Row, Nottingham, and when old could be converted into children's socks, stockings and vests.[66]

English cotton stockings were unrivalled 'for the beauty of the meshes, the material, and brightness and smoothness of the surface' in 1875 and were particularly popular in that decade in openwork or with silk embroidered clocks.[67] The French preferred their own Lisle thread hose. Some stockings had double heels and toes, probably made by plating, rendering unnecessary the careful darning of those places often done before wearing to prevent holes. In 1844 John Mercer invented a process of making cotton more susceptible to dye by passing it through caustic soda. At the end of the nineteenth century, in 1890, Horace Lowe adapted Mercer's process to make the cotton more lustrous. It was then particularly applied to Lisle stockings. Before 1900 Morley started to use the trade name 'Bombax' for cotton chemically treated to resemble silk.[68] The process was expensive but even then it threatened silk manufacture. Although it does not appear in Morley's 1902 catalogue, it is featured in the 1917 edition. By this time cotton had had to face serious competition from wool.

Dr Jaeger and wool

Wool, of course, had always been used, but in the 1880s it was pushed into prominence by Dr Jaeger's theories on healthy clothing. He advocated wool for everything; outerwear, undergarments and hosiery. In 1882 the National Health Society's exhibition in London advocated clothing which did not compress or distort the body, and was more comfortable to wear. In America the campaign had started earlier; the costume of short skirts over full trousers to the ankles, which Mrs Amelia Bloomer did not invent but promoted in her magazine *The Lily* in the 1850s, was an attempt at a more rational and comfortable dress for women, but was ridiculed to death. Trousers reappeared at the National Health Society's exhibition but as a divided skirt. Woollen 'digitated' stockings, with a separate compartment for each toe, like the fingers of gloves, were also introduced.[69] The Museum of London has a pair of cotton 'digitated' socks made by Allen, Solly & Co, and the Museum of Costume, Nottingham has a single sock by the same firm dating probably to *c* 1885.[70] The company set up by Dr Jaeger also produced such hosiery in undyed and black wool. Most seem to date, however, from about 1910. The toes are all the same size and they must have been very uncomfortable in wear. These oddities were made for men, women and children.

Men's socks

Men's socks, like women's stockings, were virtually invisible during the second half of the nineteenth century as boots were generally worn for day wear. Socks of cotton, wool, and merino (a combination of the two) were preferred, though silk was worn if it could be afforded. In the 1870s half-a-dozen pairs of hand knitted silk socks were described as a useful present to give to 'papa, to brother, or to some dear friend'. The

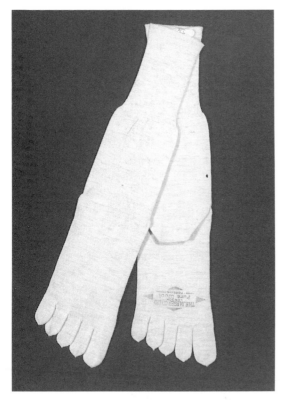

41 Man's 'digitated' socks in natural coloured wool, made and sold by Jaeger Co Ltd, c 1910; supplied with a card of wool for mending. Length 13 inches, foot length 10¼ inches

silk was obtainable in all colours and magazines frequently gave sources of supply. From the 1850s to the 1880s socks were often evenly banded, at first in two colours, or a colour and black or white, later with thin bands of more than two colours. Some had ribbed tops, and some were entirely ribbed, but with broad ribs below the tops. By 1893 the fashion for black had extended to men's socks, but by the end of the decade bright colours were being worn – scarlet, bright blue, green – sometimes to match the tie or cravat.[71] A portrait of Philip Wilson Steer by W R Sickert in about 1890 shows him wearing low-cut shoes or slippers with scarlet socks. Lytton Strachey, the writer, is wearing olive green socks with a grey suit and a green tie in his portrait of 1904 by Simon Bussy.[72] The Victoria and Albert Museum has brightly

coloured socks of this period, some embroidered, made by Morley, but plain or ribbed black or one colour socks as generally worn are not represented in this or other collections. Brightly coloured socks were popular up to World War I, particularly with the 'Knuts', middle class young 'dandies' given to wearing short trousers and shoes rather than boots.[73] A daring young man in Indianapolis in 1914 slashed his white trousers to the knee revealing red silk stockings. When arrested he demanded the same rights as women who wore the split skirt, but the women around him declared it was 'indelicate and inartistic' and hardly decent for men to show legs practically bare from the knees downwards.[74]

Men's stockings for evening and day wear

Coloured silk socks were worn with evening trousers, and even scarlet stockings with velvet breeches in the 1870s, in an attempt to brighten up men's evening dress which had otherwise fossilised into all black garments solely relieved by the white shirt.[75] Black silk socks with arrow-head clocks were usually worn. As early as 1870 Lord Leighton, the painter, and others of like mind, advocated evening dress of a black velvet or cloth tunic, knickerbockers and black silk stockings, a costume not unlike that which Oscar Wilde wore for his American tour in 1881.[76] Wilde and his affected garb were parodied in the character of Bunthorne, 'a fleshly poet', in Gilbert and Sullivan's opera Patience. Black velvet, but cut in an eighteenth century style, was later adopted instead of plum coloured cloth for civilians' suits worn at Royal Courts. Pink silk stockings were worn with the plum colour, and black ones with the velvet, but with official uniform, a gold embroidered cloth coat and white breeches, the stockings were white. In all cases the hose could be made as tights reaching to the waist; matching stockings or tights of cotton were worn underneath.

Breeches for evening wear were a continuation of eighteenth-century custom but breeches for day wear, now cut more fully and called 'knickerbockers', were a new departure. Devel-

adopted for games such as cricket, tennis, golf and football, and for cycling in the 1880s. Edward VII and George V and indeed most sportsmen wore them for shooting, with either gaiters which came up to the knees, or with spats reaching just above the ankles. In time the top of the knickerbocker stocking was decorated with pattern and colour from 1894 was hand knitted in plaid (or tartan) patterns for golf. In the same year F & W E White, of Loughborough, introduced their patent plaid half hose with lattice, diamond, and Vandyke patterns in wool or cotton, and Corah their 'Balmoral' machine knitted tartan stockings.[78]

Tartan hose

Tartan stockings were nothing new. They were worn by Highland Scots with the kilt in the eighteenth century. Then they were cut out of tartan cloth, on the bias, which gave them the characteristic diamond pattern. Hand knitted they were often of two colours only. Lord Scamperdale and Jack Spraggon wore black and white Shetland hose with suits of red and yellow 'Stunner' tartan in the early 1850s.[79] Red and black was another popular combination, and worn with matching flannel shirts, black velvet jackets, trousers and hats, by volunteer riflemen (Free Corps of Tirailleurs) at the seige of Paris in 1870.[80] Tartan stockings were particularly fashionable for women in the 1860s, worn with matching petticoats. In 1870 it was 'the correct thing' for the tartan to match the dress. Tartan reappeared as a fashionable fabric in 1884, 1893 and 1894. Stockings were either accurate copies of actual tartans, Black Watch and Royal Stuart seem to have been popular, or, especially in Paris, fancy tartans which no clan would recognise. In 1898 there seems to have been a dramatic burst of colour in stockings and tartan hose were again popular.[81] Many tartan stockings were of wool and intended for winter wear.

Children's socks and stockings

Children also wore tartan hose. In 1871 Macdougall & Co, London, advertised silk stockings

42 *A selection of evening socks, from I & R Morley's spring catalogue 1917; top left is probably shot, the rest hand embroidered; some are shown with the evening dress shoe or pump*

oped as walking dress from riding breeches in the 1850s they required a new type of stocking worn with ankle boots or stout shoes instead of top boots. These knickerbocker stockings were frequently ribbed and the top, instead of being hidden behind the kneeband of the breeches, turned down over a garter. This stocking, was often hand knitted following directions in, for example, *The Stocking Knitter's Manual* by Mrs George Cupples (1867). In 1872 a correspondent in *The Queen* advised a row of holes where the top turned down and reversing the ribs so that they would lie correctly.[77] Knickerbockers and stockings proved to be such a practical costume for anything involving movement that they were in all colours to match all tartans, as Highland costume was becoming increasingly popular for both sexes.[82] Infants, and girls up to the age of six, or sometimes later, to ten or twelve, wore socks, often of a lacy or openwork pattern, to calf height. This was a fashion first noticeable in the early nineteenth century when dresses became short enough to reveal the ankles. The fashion continued into the present century and children's socks are consequently difficult to date. White cotton was most usual but there are some charming white and pink hand knitted wool socks in the collection at Manchester. Stockings were similar to those for adults, the only difference being in the leg proportions. There seems to have been no difference in boys and girls stockings, both wore plain, ribbed, banded (often confusingly described as 'striped' in fashion reports) or tartan to match or complement the costume in the 1860s and 1870s. Boys' stockings were more conspicuous then than later on in the century as knickerbockers were generally worn for day dress. They continued to be worn for games until the turn of the century. The Duke of Windsor recalled wearing thick stockings up to the thighs with knickerbockers for football in about 1900. When he entered Osborne as a naval cadet in 1906 he had eight pairs of merino and six pairs of thick woollen socks.[83] When boys went into long trousers naturally socks like those for adults were worn. From the 1880s girls' stockings were generally black rather than matching the colour of the frock, and were even worn with white.

Suspenders and garters

In 1879 *The Milliner and Dressmaker* compared contemporary styles of children's dress with those of 1854 and commented on the simple

43   *Sir Hall Caine (1853–1931), watercolour by Sir Bernard Partridge, for* Vanity Fair, *1896. Dark coloured (black or navy blue) ribbed knickerbocker stockings with turndown tops are worn with a knickerbocker suit, turndown collar and loosely knotted tie. Sir Hall Caine was a novelist and secretary to D G Rossetti*

waistless Gabrielle styles, and practical stocking suspenders.[84] In 1877 Edwin Alexander patented shoulder straps extending below the bottom of children's stays to which the stockings could be attached.[85] Two years earlier an American invented a metal clip on the end of a strap to attach to a corset or belt to hold the stocking up.[86] The idea was taken up by the National Health Society in the 1880s. In 1884 Knights advertised The Patent Rubber Clip Stocking Suspenders, which 'cannot tear the stocking'. By 1904 the Kleinert Rubber Co were advertising a keyhole shaped loop to attach the 'Hookon' Hose supporter to a stud on a corset and in 1907 a pivot lock. The keyhole loop was also attached to the other end to fasten to the stocking over a rubber stud, the same idea was used on the Boston garter for men in 1906. Hose supporters sewn onto corsets or onto a six inch wide suspender belt were available in the 1890s.[87] Straight front corsets in 1904 had the straps attached to the front and provided the extra advantage of preventing the corset from slipping upwards. The stocking welt was made $1\frac{1}{4}$ inches deep to accommodate the suspender, and after 1900 deeper still. In 1913 The London Glove Co advertised 'Proklips' Hose (Regd No. 419444) specially designed to resist the strain of suspenders. Other forms of suspension were used: stocking tops which laced in 1884, an elastic strip attached to the corset, with a button on the end to fasten to a tape loop on the stocking in the 1890s, even sewing the stocking to the drawers, or using large safety pins.[88] Garters, however, did not immediately disappear. Silver-plated 'ventilated' garters were obtainable at 4s 6d a pair in 1876.[89] In 1886 garters had to

match the stockings and the dress and had perfumed padding under and over the knees. *The Lady's Realm* illustrates a fetching striped pair with bows and dangling pompons in 1899. The 'Keptonu' garter, patented in 1911, was made of chamois leather with pockets for cash and valuables. It cost 7s 6d, or 8s 6d with an extra large pocket. Some New York ladies did without garters or suspenders entirely by wearing socks, and probably extra long combinations, in 1897.[90] In 1913 they went a step further with the roll stocking which left the leg bare above the ankle.[91] In the same year a London business firm banned the wearing of short skirts, slashed skirts, and openwork stockings by its female staff.

Such levity disappeared with the coming of the First World War in 1914. Unlike World War II it did not greatly disrupt the hosiery industry. Young men went to war but older men were called out of retirement to man the machines and more women were recruited. Morley's 1917 catalogue is not much smaller than the 1902 edition but contains the warning that not everything might be available. The range of hosiery is still large covering every combination of fibre, pattern, style and price imaginable. In 1915 Scott & Williams' Model K circular machine could produce women's stockings from the welt to the shaped heel, toe and foot in one operation so that only the toe needed closing.[92] In the same year skirts reflected the greater freedom women were experiencing in wartime by becoming shorter. Legs were still covered out-doors by boots or gaiters, but indoors, and especially in the evening, the female leg was revealed as it never had been before.

6

1920–60

Pattern and colour in the 1920s

The short, full skirt of the war years did not last. By 1918 day dresses were long and tubular and by 1920 evening dresses had followed suit. Although skirts fluctuated in level they did not rise to any significant degree until 1925, when they reached the knee. They rarely rose above it and by 1928 evening dresses had started to descend, drooping at the back until by 1930 skirts were floor length again. Day dresses never dropped much below the lower calf in either the early 1920s or early 1930s when they were at their longest.

With long evening dresses at the beginning of the 1920s there was a revival of eccentric patterned stockings: a snake encircling the ankle, a black cat on the instep, as well as more conventional flowers in 1921.[1] But, while it was acceptable to draw attention to a shapely ankle when the rest of the leg was concealed, once more of the leg became visible the stocking became much plainer, decoration being limited to the lace clock, a double row of holes over the ankle ending in a lozenge, or the embroidered clock with the same motif in satin stitch. There were occasional exceptions. The Museum of Costume and Textiles, Nottingham, has a pair of stockings with slightly more elaborate clocks embroidered by a bride for her own wedding in 1925.[2]

Shoes and stockings had matched the evening dress in 1915 and the same rule held good into the early 1920s. Day stockings were in black or neutral shades. In 1920 the colours advertised by one firm were black, silver-grey, mole, champagne, pastille (? pastel), pink and sky (blue), and by another, black, white, grey, tan, nigger and mole.[2] Beige, grey, black and white were so

much the usual day colours in 1920 that an exception was quite startling. 'I remember the first time I saw a woman walking down the street wearing flesh-coloured ones (stockings). She was wearing a black dress that drooped at the back and was short in the front and I thought she looked quite extraordinary and just like an ostrich' (Loelia, Duchess of Westminster).[4] Flesh tones became, however, fashionable alongside the neutral shades. By 1924 nude, putty, fawn, beaver and golden tan had been added to the existing colour range, followed by sand, sunburn, and camel (1925). As colours became less adventurous their names became more so: 'Toast', 'Atmosphere', 'Piping Rock' (1925), 'Florence Mills' (after the negro star of the revue 'Blackbirds') (1927), 'Dago'. In July 1924 *The Tatler* reported: 'Stockings of an elusive dark flesh nuance – some describe them as melon colour, while others prefer to liken them to the colour of the desert women's skin – are extremely fashionable now', and more definitely in 1926: 'Various shades of sunburn stockings are worn.'[5] These deeper colours went well with sun tanned skin.

Until the early 1920s and the discovery of the health-giving properties of sunlight through the creation of vitamin D, the sun's rays were regarded with suspicion and fended off with hats, veils and parasols. In 1922 a rich American couple, Gerald and Sarah Murphy, hired a hotel for the summer on the French Riviera, hitherto a winter resort. They sunbathed and started a fashion. The sun was now welcomed. A tan implied wealth and the leisure to acquire one. Sunworshippers took the Blue Train or the Orient Express to the South of France or further afield. Some flew; others, the very rich, travelled by yacht. The complete cover-up, so much a feature

of the earlier years of the century, was utterly abandoned.

The black stocking was also being discarded. Although seen occasionally 'So unaccustomed are we to them that they give the impression that the wearer is rather a back number'.[6] Black was often worn, however, with a black evening dress, and also for mourning.

There were brief vogues for other colours. Yellow, worn with gold shoes in the evening in 1924, and light mauve stockings 'that take unto themselves a peculiar opalescent effect' when worn with silver shoes.[7] As an alternative to sunburn colour stockings, grey was worn with shoes of a darker shade in Paris, or coral-pink with black patent leather shoes, or white stockings with bronze clocks with bronze shoes, in 1926.[8] In the same year American women chose cigarettes to match their lingerie and stockings to match their face powder. 'A delicate nude tint is extremely fashionable'.[9] 'Coco' Chanel, the couturiere, in spite of being one of the first to make a suntan fashionable, preferred pale stockings even with dark colours, and her example was much copied.

Silk and artificial silk

Many of these stockings were silk, once the prerogative of the rich, now within reach of thousands of women who had earned high wages from war work. Silk stockings were a sign of prosperity, of emancipation. Their sheen drew attention to the legs, and to the shortened skirt, symbol of youth, while making the legs appear slim. Ombré stockings which were shaded from front to back were much favoured in Paris in 1925.[10] Made on a 44 gauge machine and costing £1 9s 6d a pair they were not cheap. Milanese silk stockings could cost 12s 6d, silk with Lisle feet and tops 8s 11d, mercerised Lisle 6s 6d, and fully fashioned artificial silk with Lisle feet and tops 5s 11d. Circular machine knitted artificial silk stockings were even cheaper and displaced Lisle as the less expensive alternative to silk so that Lisle, particularly in heavy weights in chocolate or mid grey tones, became associated with old ladies and schoolgirls.

44 *Black cotton stocking with elaborate decoration, probably Jacquard, 1910–20. Length 27½ inches, foot length 9 inches, 28 stitches per inch, 32 stitches per vertical inch; depth of welt 3 inches*

Artificial silk developed from the experiments with cellulose and acids in the 1880s, which resulted in explosive nitro-cellulose or gun cotton. Joseph Swan in England and the Comte de Chardonnet in France simultaneously invented methods of dissolving nitro-cellulose and extruding a thin, shiny filament which they called 'artificial silk' in 1883 and 1884.[11] Swan used his artificial silk for electric light bulb filaments, whereas Chardonnet used his for textiles. The 'cuprammonium' process, a safer way of dealing with gun cotton, was invented in Germany and the first factory to produce artificial silk by this method was in business by 1889. C H Stearn took out a British patent in 1899 to make a filament from 'viscose', cellulose treated with caustic soda. In 1904 the patent was acquired by Samuel Courtauld & Co, a firm which from the 1850s had made a fortune from rainproof mourning crepe and was now seeking to diversify as the crepe market contracted. After an initial downturn, profits from artificial silk making at their Coventry factory rose to £300,000, fifteen times the projected income in 1913.[12] By the late 1920s the term 'artificial (or art.) silk' was being replaced by the more euphonious 'rayon'. The brothers Dreyfus at the end of World War I discovered how to make another type of artificial silk by treating cellulose with acetic acid. The resultant fibre was marketed under the name 'Celanese' by the British Celanese Company.

To begin with artificial silk was often plated onto wool or cotton for strength. In 1920 such stockings cost 9s 6d a pair, but by 1926 were 2s 11d. These plated hose were both fully fashioned and seamless. In 1927 Morley's brand name for full fashioned stockings of art silk on cotton was 'Lumina', and for seamless hose of

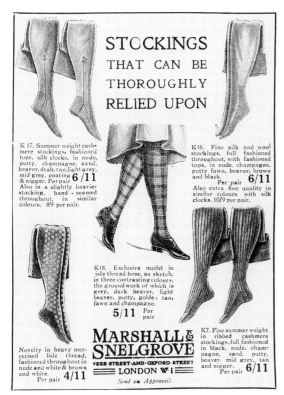

STOCKINGS
THAT CAN BE
THOROUGHLY
RELIED UPON

K17. Summer weight cashmere stockings, fashioned tops, silk clocks, in nude, putty, champagne, sand, beaver, drab, tan, light grey, mid grey, coating **6/11** & nigger. Per pair
Also in a slightly heavier stocking, hand - seamed throughout, in similar colours. 8/9 per pair.

K16. Fine silk and wool stockings, full fashioned throughout, with fashioned tops, in nude, champagne, putty fawn, beaver, brown and black. **6/11** Per pair
Also extra fine quality in similar colours with silk clocks. 10/9 per pair.

K18. Exclusive model in isle thread hose, as sketch, in three contrasting colours, the ground work of which is grey, dark beaver, light beaver, putty, golden tan, fawn and champagne.
5/11 Per pair

Novelty in heavy mercerised lisle thread, fashioned throughout in nude and white & brown and white. **4/11** Per pair

MARSHALL & SNELGROVE
VERE-STREET-AND-OXFORD-STREET
LONDON W1
Sent on Approval.

K7. Fine summer weight stockings, full fashioned in black, nude, champagne, sand, putty, beaver, mid grey, tan and nigger. **6/11** Per pair

45 *Advertisement of women's stockings, mainly for country wear, obtainable from Marshall & Snelgrove, London, from* The Gentlewoman, *26 April 1924. The colours are mainly greys and browns*

art silk on wool, 'Crystal', and 'Glistra' for the same on Sea Island cotton.[13] Seamless stockings were made on circular machines and then stretched over leg shaped boards to create their shape. After a few wearings the shaping dropped out and the stockings wrinkled around the ankles. Artificial silk was also weak when wet. Between the fully fashioned and the seamless were the stockings with mock fashioning. These had a 'seam' made by overlocking a fold in the knitting, and at intervals on each side of it, two loops caught together to make one, imitating the narrowings of fashioned hose. It can be quite difficult to distinguish between the two types, but a stocking made on a circular machine will not have a foot seam, and all the wales run vertically, regardless of the 'fashioning'. In a fashioned stocking the wales each side of the seam are vertical but the other wales join them at an angle. Morley's names for these stockings with mock marks were 'Crystalese' and 'Scintella'. The advantages of brand names, which enabled purchasers to ask for what they wanted by maker and name, were not lost on the large firms and from the early 1920s brand names became increasingly common: 'Firefly' and 'Three Knots' for instance.[14] One of the oddest was 'If Winter Comes', perhaps named after a popular novel published in 1921. These names are stamped on the side of the foot, on the toe, or on the welt. The welt itself was made much deeper to accommodate the suspender loop and stud, and much wider to fit around the thigh. Stockings with elastic tops such as 'Flexcello' and 'Wyd-Flex' brands were widely advertised.[15] Garters in the 1920s, though still used, became articles of decoration or fun, in silks or satins, with lace, floral, or diamanté trimming. Some might contain a tiny purse or a pocket for a powder-puff or mirror.[16]

Striped stockings made a comeback in the mid 1920s as wide ribs or French drop stitch Lisle hose.[17] Certain stitches in the latter were literally allowed to drop, making 'ladders', a revival of a technique used in the 1830s and 1840s for men's socks. French stockings in the inter-war period were sold by many departmental stores. French silk hose were considered to be finer,

46   *An American fashion of the mid 1920s: opaque stockings printed with a horse's head, probably visible only when the wearer sat down. Other stockings were printed with human faces below the knee. Few, if any, examples of this short-lived fashion seem to have survived.*

more stylish and generally more fashionable. Those marked 'GUI' were made by Gaston Veralier but the French sounding 'LOR' stockings were made in England.[18]

Stockings and socks for sports and games

One area in which women's stockings were rather more adventurous was in patterned hose for country wear. A glance through *The Tatler* for January to June 1926 reveals a wide variety of stockings: line checks, embroidered clocks, square checks, lattice checks, tartans and ribbed, worn with bar, lace up and ghillie shoes, often with tweed skirts. Many of the occasions reported in *The Tatler* were country race meetings and shooting parties. For many games where the clothes were plainer, black wool stockings were still worn. For rowing at Weybridge they were discarded by the women's team in 1925 with relief; 'Suspenders were very uncomfortable for

sitting on!'[19] By 1930 Morley's were selling golf and tennis socks for women. The golf socks were in shades of brown and grey, and those for tennis in white, lemon, brown or assorted colours. Both had turndown tops with fancy patterns: diced, banded, tartan, triangles, even key pattern, or club colours.

Men's hose and half-hose

Men's socks in the inter-war period echo women's hosiery; plain or a discreet pattern for formal wear, colourful patterns for informal and games wear. Evening socks were black silk or rayon, sometimes plated. The embroidered decoration on the instep gradually died out in favour of embroidered clocks in black or colour, particularly as evening pumps, low-cut with a grosgrain ribbon bow on the vamp, were giving way to patent leather Oxford shoes. Day socks for town wear, in silk, rayon, wool or Lisle were discreet in colour, navy, browns, greys, or much lighter in tone: champagne, white. If coloured socks were worn then the colour had to match or, at least tone with the tie. Georgie Pillson, in E F Benson's novel *Queen Lucia* (1920) wore with his white summer suit a mauve tie and matching socks 'so that an imaginative beholder might have conjectured that on this warm day the end of his tie had melted and run down his legs'. It was 'not done', however, to have socks, tie and handkerchief all matching. Leonard Oakroyd, a trainee barber and 'dandy', whom J B Priestley envisaged at the end of the line which began with the Macaronis, wore purple socks, tie and handkerchief with a chocolate brown suit (*The Good Companions*, 1929). Paul Alexis, a gigolo in *Have His Carcase* (Dorothy Sayers, 1932) was murdered wearing a dark blue serge suit, brown shoes and mauve socks, tie and handkerchief.

More than forty pages of Morley's 1930 catalogue are devoted to men's hose, half hose, and three-quarter hose in plain colours, fancy patterns and ribs. Every variation is here from cotton, rayon, silk, wool, Lisle, cashmere by themselves to any combination. Two tone rayon socks, for example, were available in stone colour and violet, tan and mauve, dark fawn and light purple, sandalwood and copper, with cotton tops and feet, or cotton tops and cashmere feet. Fashioned and seamless hose were offered but they varied considerably in price. Fashioned ribbed wool half hose in 6/3 rib with cards of darning wool attached cost £1 16s a dozen pairs, whereas seamless socks in 3/1 rib, in heather mixture sold at 18s 11d a dozen. Some socks were plated, some were shot (the ribs on the exterior being a different colour from those on the inside, so that when the sock was stretched the colour was visible), some were of marl cotton, two colours twisted together. Black or navy ribbed hose with coloured turnover top, often in team colours, were sold for football. Four pages

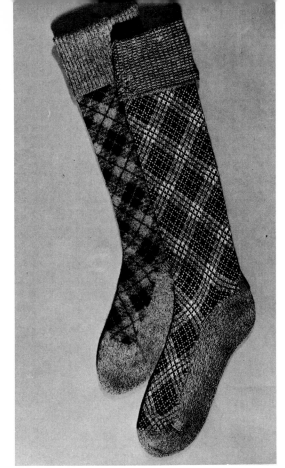

48 Men's golf stockings; with separately made sole, heel and turnover top which are machine overlocked to the argyle patterned leg. Left: worn 1920–30. Length 15½ inches, foot length 9 inches. Right: worn with a Harris Tweed plus-four suit, cap and overcoat made in 1931. Length 17 inches, foot length 10¼ inches

47 Men's fancy socks from I & R Morley's catalogue, spring 1930; all cashmere, except the last, and made on the circular machine

M 1085

M 1455

M 235

M 1475

M 1075

M 1245

were devoted to golf hose, from plain khaki, camel and white to allover patterns, the most expensive, fancy mixed, fashioned, in fine wool with turnover tops, costing £8 a dozen. The brighter, more fancy patterns of golf hose owe much to the patronage of Edward, Prince of Wales. He wore them with plus-fours (wide cut knickerbockers) and Fair Isle sweaters, fashions which were much copied.[20]

Men made no concession to the summer weather except to wear clothes of lighter colours and weight. Even for tennis white flannel trousers were worn, shorts were unheard of. An attempt was made to break down this conservatism by the formation of The Men's Dress Reform Party in 1929. Edward Shanks writing in *The Evening Standard* confessed that he would feel too self-conscious to be seen in public in the khaki shorts, the tennis shirt with open neck and rolled up sleeves, the flannel jacket, woollen stockings and worsted garters which he wore in the privacy of his own home and garden. The Cambridge branch of the MDRP pioneered a new tennis garb for men which was sold with stockings or socks with fancy tops in college colours. Dr Jordan, the Honorary Secretary, suggested a silk blouse, satin shorts and silk stockings as a suitable outfit for wear at the Cambridge May Balls in 1930.[21] The Party disbanded in 1937 without achieving any lasting changes, except perhaps in the acceptance of the wearing of shorts. Even with the popularity of suntanning it was not until after World War II that wearing ankle socks with shorts became general.

Changes during the 1930s were slight. It was fashionable in 1938 to have the golf sweater and hose to match, but the smartest combination was a navy pullover and white stockings.[22] Lastex, a rubber thread, as opposed to the strips of rubber previously used, was invented at the end of the 1920s. During the 1930s socks and stockings appear with Lastex in the ribbed tops. 'Tenova' self-supporting socks (Patent No. 323457, registered in 1929) had a band with Lastex at the top and a semi-circular cut-out below it and above the calf. Tenova Ltd held the Prince of Wales' (later King Edward VIII) warrant and socks of their manufacture still survive in the late Duke of Windsor's wardrobe at his home in Paris.[23]

Women's stockings in the 1930s

Lastex was also used in women's stockings. Munsingwear 'Knee-length' and Wayne's 'Way-nees' both had Lastex in a band at the top and were worn to just below the knee, for coolness in hot weather.[24] This was a revival in 1935 of the 'Bobbed Hosies' – knee height stockings – introduced by Phoenix, another American hosiery firm, in 1919, and was of course, only possible with longer skirts. Judging by the retail catalogues it was not a fashion adopted in Great Britain. Lastex was, however, knitted into the tops of the longer stocking but suspenders

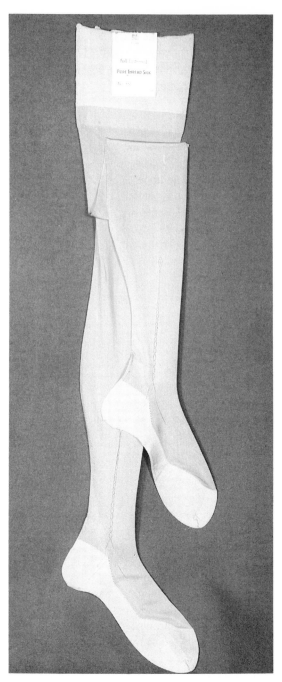

49 Stockings, 1930–40; brown silk with deep Lisle welt, shadow welt and 'cradle' sole, lace clocks, full fashioned; 'Three knots' brand, made by Wardle and Davenport Ltd, Leek; on the reverse of the label are washing instructions: 'If these instructions are followed … the permanent dull finish will be unimpaired' Length 30 inches, foot length 9½ inches

attached to the corset or a separate suspender belt were generally preferred. One fashion which was universal, however, was for dull surfaced stockings. Sheen became distinctly un-smart. Some women wore their stockings inside out, but unless the stocking was fully fashioned and hand stitched, the seam stood out as a ridge at the back of the leg. Consequently some stockings such as the Munsingwear 'Knee-length' were made inside out. Dull stockings made by Bear Brand and Morley, appear in the London Army and Navy Stores' catalogue for 1933–4.[25] Tightly twisted silk thread, such as compenzine and organzine were used for such stockings and the emphasis was on sheerness, sold as crepe-voiles, and chiffon weights. Paradoxically the dull stocking was claimed to make the leg appear slimmer.

Stockings of the 1930s incorporate numerous refinements: the long top for the suspenders, sometimes with a picot edge, a row of holes forming loops or picots, when the top was turned down, a garter or ladder stop of a lacy knit to prevent ladder going any further, the point heel which had the reinforcement of the heel coming to a point, the cradle sole, the sole reinforcement being only a thin strip along the centre to link heel and toe, and the waterproof stocking. Stockings were advertised as 'ring clear'. Three carriers were used in rotation so that the natural unevenness of the silk thread was concealed otherwise rings or bands were formed around the stocking which was particularly noticeable in sheer hose.[26] In 1935 two thread stockings were general whereas in 1925 six- or ten-thread stockings had been more usual.[27]

In 1930 Morley's claimed to make silk stockings in forty shades. Most, however, appear to be still the beige, brown, grey range. But there was a modicum of adventurousness. *Harper's Bazaar* suggested stockings packed inside wooden Russian eggs as a suitable Easter gift in 1935 and mentioned sheer blue stockings to go with navy blue clothes and those of a reddish cast 'the colour of a good West Indies sunburn' to go with sports clothes, as well as pale colours, beige and 'blue fox'.[28] In 1938 the call was for 'coppers'.[29]

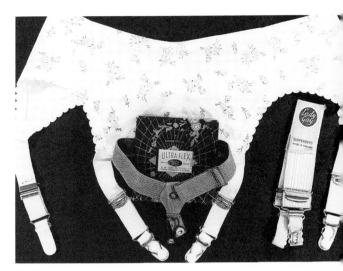

50   Keeping them up; printed cotton suspender belt, labelled 'Clarissa', 1960–70; one of a pair of men's sock suspenders and original box, 1945–50; pair of suspenders for stitching to a corset, 1950–60

Nylon

In the early 1930s rayon was dulled with metal oxides to make 'angel's skin', a smooth fibre not unlike nylon to the touch. Nylon itself was invented by E I Dupont de Nemours & Co in America in 1938. It was introduced as stockings to the American public on 'N Day', 15 May 1940 and quickly caught on.[30] Three million dozen pairs were produced in 1940, eight and a half million dozen in 1941 but only four and a half million dozen in 1942. On 7 December 1941 the Japanese bombed the American naval base at Pearl Harbour and the United States was drawn into World War II.

Thereafter nylon was used almost exclusively for military purposes, particularly for para-chutes. In a Britain already at war nylon stockings were rare, often gifts from relatives or friends in America or Canada, and were treasured. A number of museums have nylon stockings carefully hoarded from the war years. Later, American servicemen found them to be a useful form of 'currency' and to impress girls in Europe!

Hosiery in wartime

The hosiery industry was much curtailed both by staff joining the armed forces and by having to share workspace with other industries. Corah for instance lost half its workforce to the services and munitions and a third of its workspace, but still managed to produce seventeen and a half million pairs of men's socks and stockings for the war effort.[31] Cotton, rayon and wool hose were still produced for civilian use but in heavy weights to last longer. When clothes rationing was introduced in the United Kingdom in 1941, stockings rated two coupons, a dress eleven. Already worn ex-ATS stockings, refooted, or rather with the foot removed and the edges seamed, were available in Mansfield, Nottinghamshire, and probably elsewhere, for 2s 6d a pair and no coupons. Many women took to wearing ankle socks during the day, but for evening wear or special occasions, pre war stockings were hoarded and carefully repaired. A fine latch needle in a plastic handle was obtainable and in skilled hands ladders could be relooped. Women's magazines suggested ways

of making stockings last longer. Even before the war, in 1937, *The Daily Express* for 18 March carried a Parisian housewife's tips: vinegar in the rinsing water to fix the colour, methylated spirit in the second rinse to prevent spotting in the rain, face cream on the heel to prevent wear. When fine stockings were unobtainable there were various recipes for darkening the legs: permanganate of potash, walnut juice, even gravy browning, with crayons or paint or ink to draw in the seam!

Home knitting came to the fore as old woollens could be unravelled, straightened with steam and reknitted. Knitting wool spinners such as Paton and Baldwins, Sirdar, and woollen clothing manufacturers such as Viyella, Jaeger, and Bairnswear produced many patterns. So did newspapers and magazines. *The Daily Express* of 29 November 1939 printed a pattern for ankle socks, 'a necessity if you wear slacks' in moss stitch rib knitted on two needles. In December of that year *The Women's Journal* included a pattern for men's socks 'that the amateur can attempt with confidence' and Viyella advertised regulation khaki knitting wool. J D Cole of London offered a pattern for the American Swing 'Wonder-sock' (Patent No. 475912) with a separately knitted and sewn in heel and toe, which could be cut out when holey, necessitating 'no darning'.[32] Old domestic circular machines were unearthed and used again alongside the newer flat-bed machines for sock making.

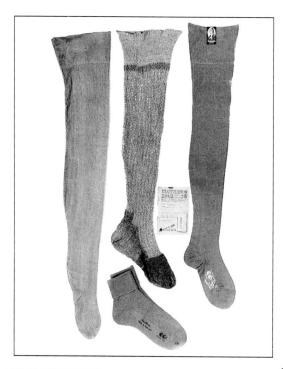

51 Women's wartime stockings:
Left: *brown Lisle, the toe and heel have been cut off, seamed under the foot, an ex ATS stocking bought for 2s 6d, 1940–45, length 28¼ inches, foot length 9 inches*
Centre: *hand knitted fawn mercerised cotton, wool top, heel and toe, 1941, length 28½ inches, foot length 10½ inches*
Right: *chocolate coloured Lisle, circular knit with mock fashioning marks; label, 'St Margaret, Regd' and Utility mark; made by Corah Ltd, Leicester, 1942–52. Length 29½ inches, foot length 8½ inches*
Socks, *fawn wool, Utility mark, 1942–52; clothing ration book, 1947–8, one of the last, most of its pages are complete*

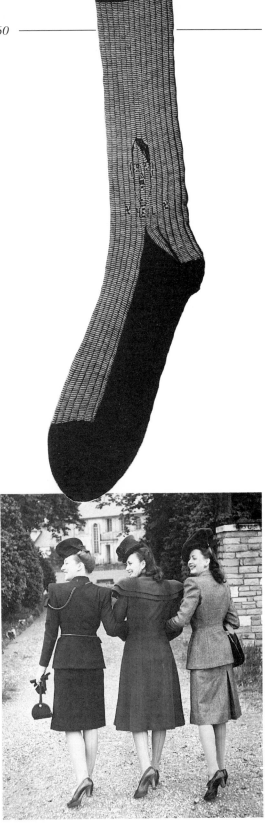

Hosiery in the post war period

After the war normality returned slowly. The Utility Scheme (established by the Civilian Clothing Act in 1941) which set standards for the manufacture of clothes, continued until 1952. Clothes rationing ceased in 1948. Many firms' products were intended primarily for export, to bring much-needed foreign money into the country, with home needs coming a very poor second. Nylon stockings, or 'nylons' as they were now generally known, were available in restricted quantities from 1947, otherwise chiffon weight Lisle stockings were worn in preference to rayon.[33] Wolsey advertised export only nylons in fashion shades such as 'Fervent', 'Blythe', 'Idyll' and 'Enchant' in 1950, but by 1952 they were plentiful enough for British Nylon Spinners, a combination of Imperial Chemical Industries and Courtaulds Ltd, to place information advertisements in such magazines as *Vogue* and *Harpers' Bazaar*. Denier, the measurement of the thickness of thread, now entered the fashion conscious woman's vocabulary. Nylon was available in 15 denier (very fine) and 30 denier (medium fine) in 45, 48, 51, 54, 60 or 66 gauge in plain, mesh, or lace knits. The finest stockings were fully fashioned, 15 denier, 66 gauge.[34] By 1955 Vayle and Taylor-Woods were producing 75 gauge stockings in 12 denier nylon. After the anarchy of wartime fashions there were almost rigid rules as to what could be worn with what and manufacturers stressed the occasions for which the different qualities would be suitable. The finest stockings were for evening wear, particularly with the short evening dress for cocktail parties, which had become the most fashionable way of entertaining after the war.

52 **Top right:** *'Hitler' sock, 1939–45, black and white wool, with Hitler's face, 'Heil' and two swastikas at the ankle, made by Allen, Solly & Co Ltd. There was also, apparently, a Churchill sock. Length 15 inches, foot length 10½ inches*

53 *Women's seamed stockings, from 'Britain's Best Clothes Are for Export', a feature in* Picture Post, *21 July 1945*

54   Men's socks, argyle pattern (by Jacquard), in grey, white and red wool; Utility mark; possibly by Rowley & Co Ltd, Leicester, 1942–52

Fully fashioned, the most desirable of nylon stockings, were now made in one piece on the machine, abandoning William Cotton's separate machines for legs, feet, and sometimes welts. New machines formed a heel which was made at an angle to the main fabric while the needles knitting the leg marked time.[35] This heel had an underfoot seam and dispensed with the heel flaps. The fully fashioned market in America rose from 15 per cent of total production in 1919 to 87.3 per cent in 1952.[36] Machines increased in speed from 40 rows per minute in 1900 to 100 in 1954. Initially there were problems with length. It was possible for two stockings knitted on the same machine to differ by as much as four inches in length. In 1952 under the guidance of HATRA (the Hosiery and Allied Trades Research Association) means were found to regulate machines to 1/10,000″ accuracy and to measure the stocking as it was made.[37]

The fashionable sheer stocking was made still in shades of brown and grey. In 1947 coloured heel and toes to stockings were recommended wear in America with open sandals; *Housewife* suggested brightly coloured cross stitches at the heel and toe as a British alternative.[38] Sheer stockings with black heels, toes and seams were available in the mid 1950s but many women considered them to be in doubtful taste, and positively disapproved of those with rhinestones down the back seam. Coloured bands were used by Ballito in 1955 as a coding device for different qualities of stocking: white for evening hose, yellow for 'Afternoons and After Five', blue for town wear, and red for tweeds and country clothes. Nylon is thermoplastic which means that it can be permanently set to shape by heat. This was particularly useful for circular knits and gave nylon a decided advantage over cotton and rayon. The fashion for the nude look, a seamless circular knit with no mock-fashioning marks, in 1954 exploited this characteristic and marked the beginning of the end for the fully fashioned stocking.[39]

Although nylons were the favourites, silk stockings were still made but in lessening quantities. Wool, in black, was popular with the arty 'Chelsea set' in the late 1950s, but in fancy patterns for country wear was being threatened by spun nylon lace patterned stockings made under the name 'Martyn Fisher' by B Walton & Co of Sutton-in-Ashfield, Nottinghamshire, and by crepe nylon, a bulkier, more matt form of the fibre with terrific stretch potential. Crepe and spun nylon were popular for men's socks, in all sorts of ribbed patterns and colours. Harrods *News for Men*, Spring 1955, advertised crepe nylon socks in grey, blue, beige, mulberry, yellow, or black from 11s 6d plain to 14s 6d fancy. Short socks were one shilling cheaper, and ribbed wool socks, reinforced with nylon, were 10s 6d a pair, in clerical or steel grey, brown, wine, navy or black. Socks in pure cotton and Lisle or with the addition of Terylene, the brand name of polyester discovered by the Calico Printers Association in 1941, were still available. Both Terylene and acrylic fibres, developed by Courtauld, were heavily promoted in the mid 1950s. Man-made fibres seemed to herald a new, a modern age.

7
1960–90

Women's stockings in the 1950s and 1960s

Whereas the 1950s had been the era of the sedate young matron, perhaps in reaction to the unsettling effect of the war, the 1960s, particularly the last years, was the era of the young. The mini-skirt seems to dominate the decade but it did not appear until 1964 when André Courreges raised the hemline to four inches above the knee, and did not reach its most abbreviated form until 1967. The earlier 1960s were a continuation of the 1950s in style of dress but in stockings there were the beginnings of a change.

Micromesh and lace patterned stockings, as well as plain, has been worn throughout the 1950s. Micromesh had every loop or second loop taken over two needles, locking the threads so that if they were snagged they went into holes rather than ladders, and as such they were popular for everyday wear. They resembled irregular net in appearance. Lace patterns were small and discreet, but in the 1960s they became larger. In an advertisement for shoes of black leather with stacked heels and ankle straps, designed by Mary Quant, the lacy stockings patterned with hexagons have prominence. These were not a Quant design as she did not start designing hosiery until 1965.[1]

The lacy patterns were in the knit of the stocking (rather than of machine made lace as are recent stockings) and were often small, geometric motifs, such as hexagons, lozenges and squares, which became larger towards the end of the decade.

Stockings of the early 1960s were worn with shoes with sharply pointed toes and high thin heels. As skirts rose the toe became broader and the heel lower and more square, as if echoing the broad-toed shoes worn by children. At the same time, with the fashion for bobbed hair and the emphasis on youth, there were elements of a return to the 1920s in style, but a 1920s much more vivid and lively especially where stockings were concerned. Stockings in general became thicker and the lace patterns more obtrusive. Prices ranged from £4 10s for hand knitted stockings from Women's Home Industries, through black seamed lacy stockings by Balenciaga at £1 10s 6d and 'Cobweb' stockings by Bonnie Doon in bronze green, periwinkle blue, blonde, cranberry red and black at £1 1s 6d to ribbed stockings by Corah at 9s 11d in 1965. In January of that year Mary Quant broke away from abstract patterns to make stockings with floral sprigs and by September 1967 had produced tights with her famous daisy logo.[2] She was among the first dress designers to design hosiery. Others followed suit, or had hosiery made to sell under their names, particularly now because the visible length of leg could make a fashion statement. Christian Dior and Norman Hartnell stockings were readily available, the former in grey packaging, the latter in a distinctive pink. They were attempts by established dress designers to capitalise on their names and to seek a way into the mass market. (The designer fetish was carried to ridiculous extremes in the 1980s when everything had to have a 'designer' label.) In catering for such a market exclusivity was lost, and with it the dictatorship of the fashion houses.

Hosiers tackled the mass market from other directions: livelier designs and in 1967 the introduction by Pretty Polly of one size stockings, followed in 1968 by one size tights.[3]

Tights

Tights were the answer to a practical problem as more of the thighs became visible. Alternatives had been tried: dress and knickers of matching material, very reminiscent of small girls' clothes of the 1920s, and Kayser's 'Topics' with floral or lace printed tops.[4] Pretty Polly's 'Hold-ups' in 1967, had an elasticated band at the top, and did away with the suspender belt, which was all too visible under the shift-like dress. But for modesty tights were the obvious solution. Tights in this context meant allover leg covering from waist to toe. Tights in this style had been made for theatrical wear in wool and cotton from the early nineteenth century onwards. White and Sons of Bobbers Mill, Nottingham, were particularly famous for tights and other stage hosiery. Theatrical tights were tried under mini-skirts but they were thick and opaque and not very successful. Hosiery manufacturers were soon producing sheer tights in nylon. These were knitted as tubes, slit and U seamed to make tights or 'pantyhose'. In 1968 Charnos was advertising 'Hold-Me-Tights', tights with a built-in girdle, said to 'stay put no matter what'.[5] By 1972 much of the construction of pantyhose was done automatically. A further extension of the stocking was the 'Body-stocking' introduced by Warners in 1965. But covering the body as it did, it was not so practical as tights.

The success of tights almost extinguished the production of stockings. But there was competition in the form of the boot. The couturier Courreges included calf-high white boots in his collection in 1964. They, in their turn, were said to have been inspired by British women wearing boots during the severe winter of 1963.[6] The fashion boot varied in height from just above the ankle to mid-thigh level and was made in leather, suede and various plastics. Worn with the mini-skirt a lot of leg was still visible, but the mini itself faced competition from the 'maxi-look' in 1969 and went out of main stream fashion in the early 1970s. But the boot remained, and was especially popular with the frilled cotton skirts which were part of an 'American pioneer' or 'Russian' look, depending on one's viewpoint, and a reaction to synthetics as the rising price of oil reduced their cheapness. Unfortunately for the manufacturers this fashion left nothing of the hose visible.

Tights face competition

Competition also came from trousers which had only recent become an accepted part of women's wear. Slacks worn for sports such as sailing had developed from beach pyjamas during the 1930s, and during World War II were found to be a practical alternative to the skirt in active work. In America during the 1950s jeans, made of denim, a particularly hardwearing blue and white cotton cloth, had become general leisure wear, as opposed to purely working garments, for both sexes. Mary Quant introduced them in her 1963 collection. Courreges showed sequinned evening trousers in 1964, and by 1968 trousers were teamed with wide lapelled jackets as trouser suits for women. In contrast to men, women were prepared to wear more exciting socks with their trousers. Mary Quant designed red and white banded socks, brassiere and briefs for wear with jeans in 1965.[7] But trousers, jeans and boots dealt a severe blow to the market for tights. In January to June 1976 only twenty one million dozen pairs of tights were produced compared with fifty two million dozen in 1972.[8] By 1977 the annual total was less than forty million dozen, also there was the threat from Italian competition.[9]

Shoes in the early 1970s were platform soled, and thick square or wedge heeled. The tights worn with them were often sheer or semi-sheer in colours, made in one of the improved nylons, such as 'Celon' or 'Cantrece'. Sometimes they were thicker, in wool or substitutes, and ribbed; Jap, of Jap and Joseph, teamed a white wrap-round mini-skirt with beige wool ribbed tights, blue ankle socks and blue suede sandals in September 1976.[10] Socks to the knee, with or without turnover tops, in lattice or diamond patterns, or in chunky knits, such as cabling, were very popular as they could be worn with skirts, shorts or trousers. Colour was otherwise brought to the leg by 'leg warmers', footless stockings with bands of ribbing at the top and bottom; originally worn by ballet dancers to keep the legs warm during rehearsals. A pair, banded in purple, beige, wine, green and orange wool, were available from Charles Jourdain for £8.50 in 1977.[11] They, along with footless tights, became a staple part of young women's wardrobes, of practical as well as decorative use as more women went to exercise classes, aerobic and otherwise. In September 1978 *Cosmopolitan* recommended in its Fashion Checklist: 'Buy at least one pair of leggings or footless tights and belt your dresses over the top'.[12]

The return of the stocking

Shoes began to lose their thick and heavy appearance in about 1976, heels grew higher and more slender, toes more almond shaped. Dresses and jackets became squarer at the shoulders and by 1979 some skirts were split at the side. In 1977 stockings made a come-back and were especially popular with girls who had grown up since the advent of tights and to whom suspender belts were sexy rather than just a means of holding up the stockings. The suspender belt itself was softer and more comfortable to wear.[13] Aristoc made stockings which were black with a seam, and a point to the reinforcement at the heel for 75p a pair. They were regarded as part of the nostalgic vogue for the clothes of the 1940s, hence the square shoulders. However, the shoes they were teamed with were revivals of the 1960s stiletto, which became the minimalised sandals of high heel, sole and thin straps in the 1980s. Brettles also made stockings in a thick lacy knit, not unlike the hand knit stockings of the war years, and in 1988 Pretty Polly produced 'Nylons' a conscious attempt to re-create the look and feel of early nylons but with Lycra as well as nylon.[14] Tights were still the most popular with stockings accounting for only six to eight per cent of the market in 1980.[15] It rose to ten per cent in 1984 and in 1988 it was reckoned that women under the age of twenty-five bought one pair of stockings to every three pairs of tights.[16] On average every woman bought twenty-three pairs of stockings and tights

per year. The fashion for stockings was primarily a British one; not even the French liked them so well.

Tights and socks in the 1970s and 1980s

The increasing affluence of many women in the 1970s and 1980s coupled with an independence of spirit engendered by the feminist movement, created a fragmentation of fashion. Women were encouraged by the fashion magazines to develop their own individual styles, to look good in their own eyes rather than other peoples and to follow their own fashion sense. Hosiery manufacturers tried to anticipate the new trends with more variety and higher quality. Pretty Polly identified five looks in its advertising campaign of Spring 1987 – rebel 'bold and animated', mirage shimmering with 'texture', cosmetique 'feminine and pretty', oceanique 'casual but body conscious', and exotique 'rich, orientally luxurious' – each with up to four colours of tights.[17]

Tights had started to become more decorative in the late 1970s, at first with discreet spots in black and white, then in ten bright colours, with sparkling gold, silver and 'Bermuda blue' for parties. Ankle decoration re-emerged in 1980, and in 1983 a diaper of green and pink tulips on a white, blond, or cloud ground ('Paloma Mink' was the most popular colour in that year) made by Kunert from a design by David and Elizabeth Emmanuel, designers of the Princess of Wales' wedding dress in 1981.[18] The Princess herself boosted the demand for decorative tights by wearing a pair with bows on the back seams above the shoe, the first time that attention had been drawn to this area. Patterned tights became big news in 1985. Pretty Polly introduced their 'Creations' range of patterned and lacy tights, the latter made of stretch lace, cut and sewn to shape, Elbeo black tights with scarlet seams, and Aristoc stockings and tights in 'Daisy Dot' patterns in pink, mint, carnation, apricot, brilliant white and shades of cream. Pretty Polly's range of colours in 15 denier tights in the years 1986 to 1987 ran to forty five, decreasing to twenty two in 1989, a contrast to the eight available in the 1970s.[19]

By 1986 patterns were exotic: rainbow or tie-and-dyed; stamped in gold with leaves or peacocks; printed with flowers, both natural and stylised, or tigers; in bands reminiscent of the 1860s or tartans reminiscent of the 1890s; with spots, lozenges, even alphabets and flags. Almost anything went as long as it drew attention to the legs. Prices ranged from £27 for a pair of Pierre Mantsux tights with gold seams and diamanté tassels to less than £1.[20] Many of the new styles were made possible by the use of computerised machines developed in Italy and Japan.

Computers were also used in the production of colourful socks in up to nine colours in fine gauges. It takes twenty minutes to feed in a pattern compared with the three days necessary to do the work manually, and the design potential is unlimited. Unlike tights which are made as tubes with no heels and little in the way of a toe, socks have both, with a seam across the top of the toes. Socks, ankle and knee heights in bright colours or textured were fashionable in 1982, worn with knickerbockers or Bermuda shorts or the revived mini-skirt. By 1985, as with tights, anything was acceptable, from animals, to aircraft, to alphabets.[21]

Men's hose

Men's socks also underwent a form of liberation in the 1980s. In the 1960s they were much as they had been in the 1950s. The emphasis was still on nylon in a great many Jacquard patterns as being easy to wash and hard wearing, although many men found it uncomfortable to wear for any length of time. Nylon was also used to reinforce woollen socks. Colours were mostly subdued. Only 'Teddy Boys' in the mid 1950s dared to wear luminous yellow socks with crepe rubber soled shoes and tight 'drainpipe' trousers.[22] Tight trousers were also a feature of

55 *Sideline net hold-ups from Pretty Polly's first Creations range in 1985. They were available in Chintz, Pink Orchid, Paprika and white and retailed at £2.50. The Creations range was designed by Emilio Cavallini and included lace, patterned and motif tights and stockings.*

56 *Selection of men's socks in nylon and terylene, variously coloured grey and cream, grey and fawn, green and fawn, green and cream and black and cream; made by Byford & Co Ltd of Leicester, 1957*

the 'Italian' look in the late 1950s and early 1960s. Worn with sharply pointed, cuban heeled, elastic sided Chelsea boots little, if anything, of the socks was visible. The late 1960s and early 1970s saw an explosion of colour and pattern in men's wear, not only in shirts and ties but in suitings as well. Flared trousers were worn with square toed, platform soled shoes, and brightly coloured socks. Wolsey still made long socks in neutral shades with a distinctive red band at the top, but in 1970 they produced entirely scarlet socks for men. In 1971 unisex fashions brought forth tights for men, the 'Bobby Moore Action Pants' made by Sunarama in black, brown, navy, stone, burgundy, moss green, and purple nylon rib, with a zipped fly.[23] Though undoubtedly warm, they were likened to old fashioned 'long johns' – drawers which reached from waist to ankle – and were probably limited to sports wear. Sports socks, particularly in terry knit, were popular wear with track suits and training shoes when adopted for day wear. ICI's 'natural' look for 1973 with wool, linen, cotton and silk being imitated in Terylene, Bri-nylon, Terylene/viscose and Bri-nova, was followed towards the end of the 1970s, as rising oil prices forced up the cost of synthetics, by natural fibres and a revival of cotton for socks.[24]

57 Men's stockings for sport: Left: Jacquard pattern in navy blue, pale blue and brick red acrylic imitating wool, elasticated band of ribbing at top; worn for cycling 1960–70. Length 16½ inches, foot length 9 inches Right: cream wool with coloured flecks, circular knit, deep ribbed cuff, ribbing at top of foot and ankle for better grip; worn for walking and hill climbing, 1970–80. Length 20½ inches, foot length 9¼ inches

The most general fashion in recent years is the wearing of brilliant white socks with black slip-on shoes.

During the 1980s there have been many 'fun' socks with abstract or other designs, intended to be worn for a few occasions and then discarded. Menswear designers, such as Paul Smith, have only recently turned their attention to socks. The Victoria and Albert Museum has a pair made in 1984 in turquoise and pink mercerised cotton with an ethnic pattern by Paul Smith, and two pairs of Giani Versace socks, one in thick ribbed white cotton with fawn tops, ankles and toes, the other in black with skiers in khaki down the sides.[25] Men in general being conservative, patterns are discreet. Even so many men still regard any pattern as anathema and opt for plain coloured ribbed socks, in accordance with, largely unwritten, 'laws' of smart dressing.

The Duke of Windsor commented on the different 'laws' of the British and the Americans in 1960. He himself wore tie, shirt, socks and handkerchief to tone more or less with his suit, but noticed that Americans either wore them all different at one extreme, or, at the other, shirt, tie and handkerchief of the same checked pattern. He also noted that New York businessmen wore black socks to the office, 'such as I myself wear with evening dress alone'.[26] Black silk socks reaching to mid-calf or above, 'Since seeing a male shin, horror of horrors, is supposed to be gauche' were recommended for evening dress by Charles Hix in Dressing Right (1978).[27] Sock colour should either match the shoes or the trousers. 'The most absolutist [sic] concept is that socks should pick up some color texture or pattern from the shirt or tie.'[28] Both the British and Americans tend to wear plain colours, 'heather mixtures', ribs and argyles, with the British also preferring marled colours, textured patterns or cables. Europeans on the other hand preferred dark colours, finer textures, ribs, diamond self-patterns and embroidered clocks.

The selling of hosiery

Socks are still purchased mainly from outfitters and departmental stores, and also by mail order, as indeed they have been since the beginning of the century. Carl Freschl advertised boxes of three pairs of men's hole-proof socks or ladies' stockings at 9s or 12s 6d, and Jason's of Leicester gift boxes of two or three pairs of stockings or socks for 3s 11d in 1914.[29] Peter Robinson offered six pairs of silk stockings in a cretonne covered box for £3 5s or £3 15s in 1918.[30] Stockings in paper covered boxes feature in the Christmas gift catalogues of the London departmental stores of Derry and Toms and Swan and Edgar in the 1930s. Stockings were sold in paper and cellophane envelopes in the 1930s, followed after the World War II by polythene and various transparent plastics. As the importance of stylish presentation was realised, the packaging became almost more attractive than the contents. Since super-stretch nylon and one size tights in the late 1960s, women's tights have been available in super-markets and corner shops. This is not so surprising. Hosiery is virtually the only fashion item which receives the same sort of press and television advertising as instant coffee or a chocolate bar. In 1972 Pretty Polly launched the Galaxy range of tights specifically for supermarkets which, by 1980, claimed forty per cent of the industry's total sales.[31]

At the other end of the scale was the Sock Shop, set up by Sophie Mirman and her husband, Richard Ross, to sell a wide range of hosiery but chiefly socks. From one shop in 1983 they expanded to over a hundred outlets in 1990. An exhibition at the Victoria and Albert Museum in 1989 featured socks by Betty Jackson, Artwork, Workers for Freedom, Jasper Conran and English Eccentrics, as well as rainbow, tie-dyed, lace and printed tights, all produced for Sock Shop. Too rapid expansion, coupled with overstocking and borrowed money, a mild winter followed by a hot summer caused the collapse of the Sock Shop chain.[32] By July 1990 Mirman and Ross had left and the business with a reduced number of outlets was acquired by a consortium.

As the 1980s gave place to the 1990s the variety of socks, stockings and tights could hardly be bettered. Colours were tied in to the fashion colours of the season and patterns varied with the season. As a balance, black made a come-back in thick, opaque tights worn with high-heeled shoes or rather mannish lace-ups. Worn by the young they can be seen as an echo of 1950s' beatnik rebellion re-interpreted by Japanese minimalist designers, such as Rei Kawakubo at Comme Des Garçons or even of the passion for black at the end of the nineteenth century.

The traditional emphasis on fineness and fit meant a denier decrease from 15 in 1977 to 10 in 1978, 7 in 1982 and 5 in 1990, and the greater use of 'Lycra', an elastane fibre developed by Du Pont de Nemours International in the 1950s.[33] It was used initially in corsetry and surgical support hose, but by 1982 it was made sufficiently fine for its stretch and support properties to be found of benefit even in fashion stockings, and now a significant proportion of

58   *Motif tights in the After Dark range by Pretty Polly, 1989. The motif, in nylon flock, is heatbonded to the fabric; diamanté adds sparkle.*

women's hosiery contains it. For the traditionalist, silk stockings made a come-back in the 1970s and can now be found in departmental stores. Better and faster machines have meant hosiery can be produced in seconds rather than minutes and to the traditional hosiery producing centres have been added Japan, Korea and China.

As the story of machine knitted hosiery begins with William Lee, it may be considered appropriate to end with him. In 1989, during the quatercentenary year of the invention of the stocking frame, Her Majesty Queen Elizabeth II was graciously pleased to accept a pair of stockings from British hosiers, a gesture that neatly refuted Queen Elizabeth I's rejection of Lee. These and the other commemorative stockings were made in white nylon, with a special scalloped top and a welt with the Royal Cipher, dates and quatercentenary logo, on modern circular machines, and encapsulated both the debt to William Lee and the advance of the present day hosiery industry.

Notes and References

Chapter 1

1 N B HARTE, 'William Lee and the Invention of the Knitting Frame', in *Four Centuries of Machine Knitting*, ed J MILLINGTON and S CHAPMAN, Knitting International, Leicester, 1989, pp 17–18

2 See G HENSON, *The History of the Framework Knitters . . .*, 1831, David & Charles reprints, 1970, ch II, pp 38–52, and W FELKIN, *History of the Machine-wrought Hosiery and Lace Manufactures*. Longmans, Green & Co, London, 1867, ch III & IV, pp 23–58

3 E PASOLD, In Search of William Lee, *Textile History*, Vol 6, 1975, pp 12–13

4 PASOLD, op cit, p 11

5 R RUTT, *A History of Hand Knitting*, Batsford, 1987, p 39

6 Ibid. pp 39–44

7 For instance in Tinn, Telemark, Norway, where knitted stockings were worn only on Sundays, see A NOSS, 'With One Foot in the Middle Ages . . .', *Costume* 23, 1989, pp 22–38; also C HAWKINS, 'A Fifteenth Century Pattern for "chausses" . . .', *Costume* 6, 1972, pp 84–85

8 RUTT, op.cit. p 80

9 J STOW, *The Annales or Generall Chronicle of England*, quoted in M GRASS, *A History of Hosiery*, Fairchild Publications, 1955, pp 120–1

10 RUTT, op.cit. p 68

11 C H ASHDOWN, *British Costume during XIX centuries*, Nelson, c1920, p 215

12 A J CARTER, 'Mary Tudor's Wardrobe', *Costume* 18, 1984, p 25

13 Middleton Manuscripts, *Report of the Historical Manuscripts Commission*, 1911 (for WILLOUGHBY) and A BUCK, 'The Clothes of Thomasine Petre', 1555–1559, *Costume* 24, 1990, p 21

14 *The Milliner & Dressmaker*, Dec. 1875, p 21

15 STOW, op.cit. in GRASS, op.cit. p 134

16 Ibid. pp 120–121

17 J ARNOLD *Queen Elizabeth's Wardrobe Unlock'd*, W S MANEY, Leeds, 1988, p 208

18 RUTT, op.cit. p 66

19 STOW, op.cit. in GRASS, op.cit. p 120

20 ARNOLD, op.cit. p 208

21 C W & P CUNNINGTON, *A Handbook of English Costume in the Sixteenth Century*, Faber & Faber, 1954, p 181

22 ARNOLD, op.cit. p 206

23 RUTT, op.cit. pp 71–2, and ARNOLD, op.cit. pp 207–8

24 cf ARNOLD, op.cit. pp 206–10

25 CUNNINGTON, op.cit p 35

26 Illustrated in colour in RUTT, op.cit. plate 4

27 Quoted in F W FAIRHOLT, *Costume in England*, Chapman & Hall, second edition, 1860, p 591

28 G EKSTRAND, 'Some Early Silk Stockings in Sweden', *Textile History*, Vol 13 (2), 1982, pp 166–168

29 I TURNAU, 'Stockings from the Coffins of the Pomeranian Princes', *Textile History*, Vol 8, 1977, pp 167–9

30 and 31 Lord Middleton Collection Nos 22 & 30

32 Victoria and Albert Museum negative 70976; see W H ST J HOPE and J A ROBINSON, 'On the funeral effigies of the Kings and Queens of England . . . in the Abbey Church of Westminster', *Archaeologia*, Vol 60, 1907, p 557

33 W LARKIN portrait at Ranger's House, Blackheath, London; I OLIVER portrait in the Victoria and Albert Museum, accession No. P721-1882; portrait of Dudley, 3rd Baron North, also Victoria and Albert Museum, cf V CUMMING, *A Visual History of Costume: the Seventeenth Century*, Batsford, 1984, plate 17

34 P & A MACTAGGART, 'The Rich Wearing Apparel of Richard, 3rd Earl of Dorset', *Costume* 14, 1980, pp 41–55

35 Accession No. T126-1938

36 No. 3381; coronation stockings of 1617 are No. 3378; see EKSTRAND, op.cit. pp 168–70

37 F MORYSON, *An Itinerary*, quoted in N WAUGH, *The Cut of Men's Clothes, 1600–1900*, Faber & Faber, 1964, p 43

38 R STRONG, 'Charles I's Clothes for the Years 1633 to 1635', *Costume* 14, 1980, pp 73–89

39 For tennis socks see unidentified portrait *c* 1720 in P CUNNINGTON & A MANSFIELD, *English Costume for Sports and Outdoor Recreation*, A & C Black, 1969, plate 16

40 CUNNINGTON, op.cit. p 37

41 W FELKIN, op.cit. p 60

42 Illustrated in P LEWIS, 'William Lee's Stocking Frame . . . 1589–1750', *Textile History* Vol 17(2), 1986, pp 130–134

43 C W & P CUNNINGTON, *A Handbook of English Costume in the Seventeenth Century*, Faber & Faber, 1955, pp 64–5

44 Ibid. p 161

45 FAIRHOLT, op.cit. pp 247–8

46 S PEPYS, Diary, entry for 29 November 1663

47 See painting of 1647 by HIERONYMUS JANSSENS in P THORNTON, *Authentic Decor . . . 1620–1920*, Weidenfeld & Nicolson, 1984, p 39

48 J EVELYN, Diary, quoted in WAUGH, op.cit. p 48

49 CUNNINGTON, op.cit. p 189

50 J KENDALL, 'The Development of a Distinctive Form of Quaker Dress', *Costume* 19, 985, p 60

51 EKSTRAND, op.cit. p 171–4

52 I ANTHONY, 'Clothing Given to a Servant . . .', *Costume* 14, 1980, pp 37–40

Chapter 2

1 N WAUGH, *The Cut of Women's Clothes, 1600–1930*, Faber & Faber, 1968, p 52
2 N WAUGH, *The Cut of Men's Clothes, 1600–1900*, Faber & Faber, 1964, pp 45–6
3 J THIRSK, 'The Fantastical Folly of Fashion' in *Textile History and Economic History; Essays in Honour of Miss Julia de Lacy Mann*, ed N B HARTE and K G PONTING, Manchester University Press, 1973, pp 61–2
4 *The Journeys of Celia Fiennes*, ed C MORRIS, Cresset Press, 1949, pp 150, 234
5 D DEFOE, *A Tour Through the Whole Island of Great Britain*, Penguin, 1971, pp 207, 366
6 Ibid. p 513
7 Ibid. p 655
8 Accession No. T638A-1910
9 M DUNLEVY, *Dress In Ireland*, Batsford, 1989, pp 81–2; James I and Duchess of Richmond and Lennox stockings, Victoria and Albert Museum negatives 70976 and 69605, see also L E TANNER and J L NEVINSON, 'On Some Later Funeral Effigies in Westminster Abbey', *Archaeologia*, Vol 85, 1936, pp 178–9
10 Quoted in C W & P CUNNINGTON, *A Handbook of English Costume in the Seventeenth Century*, Faber & Faber, 1955, p 161
11 T175-1900, Victoria and Albert Museum
12 DEFOE, op.cit. p 214
13 R CAMPBELL, *The London Tradesman*, London, 1747, p 215
14 See P LEWIS, 'William Lee's Stocking Frame', *Textile History*, Vol 17(2), 1986, pp 129–147
15 W FELKIN, *History of the Machine-wrought Hosiery and Lace Manufactures*, Longmans, Green & Co, 1867, p 69
16 Ibid. p 71
17 See painting by HENRI TESTELIN, tapestry after CHARLES LE BRUN and painting by ANTOINE VAN DER MEULEN, all at the Musée de Versailles
18 THIRSK, op.cit. p 59
19 C GULVIN, 'The Origins of Framework Knitting in Scotland', *Textile History*, Vol 14 (1), 1983, pp 58–9
20 M SONENSCHER, 'The Hosiery Industry of Nîmes and the Lower Languedoc in the Eighteenth Century', *Textile History*, Vol 10, 1979, p 142
21 I TURNAU, 'Aspects of the Russian Artisan...', *Textile History*, Vol 4, 1973, p 13
22 Ibid. pp 15–16
23 E SANDERSON, 'The Edinburgh Milliners, 1720–1820', *Costume 20*, 1986, p 23
24 Quoted in N WAUGH, *The Cut of Men's Clothes, 1600–1900*, Faber & Faber, 1964, p 100
25 M EVELYN, *Mundus Muliebris*, ed J NEVINSON, Costume Society Extra Series 5, 1977
26 Lord Middleton Collection No. 49
27 Accession No. NCM 1985-770/1
28 Victoria and Albert Museum negative 68312; see L E TANNER and J L NEVINSON, op.cit. p 182
29 G HENSON, *History of the Framework Knitters*, 1831, David & Charles. 1970, pp 211–2
30 Accession No. PH 178
31 Accession Nos 1947.1917, 1976.125
32 Accession No. A15100
33 C W & P CUNNINGTON, *A Handbook of English Costume in the Eighteenth Century*, Faber & Faber, 1957, p 396
34 H WILSON, *Memoirs of Herself and Others*, 1825, Davies, London, 1929, pp 579, 412
35 DUNLEVY, op.cit. pp 84–5
36 *World of Fashion*, Vol II, 1825, pp 376–7
37 W GARDINER, *Music and Friends*, 1838, Vol I, p 91
38 *An Inventory of the Wardrobe of the Rt Honble ye Marquis of Carmarthen; taken July ye 5th 1728*, Yorkshire Archaeological Society, Duke of Leeds Collection DD5/35. I am indebted here to Nicholas Brewster and Avril Hart
39 F W FAIRHOLT, *Costume in England*, Chapman & Hall, second edition, 1860, p 275
40 DUNLEVY, op.cit. p 92
41 W HOGARTH, *The Rake's Progress*, Sir John Soane's Museum, London, illustrated in colour in *Manners and Morals, Hogarth and British Painting, 1700–60*, Tate Gallery exhibition catalogue, 1987, pp 98–101, plates 77–80
42 W HOGARTH, *Times of Day*, Grimsthorpe and Drummond Castle Trustees, illustrated in colour, ibid. plate 92, p 110
43 Portrait by LOUIS-GABRIEL BLANCHET, National Portrait Gallery London, No. 5517
44 E.g., T1720-1913 Victoria and Albert Museum; A12418, A12544, Museum of London
45 P BYRDE, *The Sir Thomas Kirkpatrick costume*, in the National Art Collection Fund Review, 1986, pp 112–3
46 For example C TROOST, *Governors of the Orphanage*, mid 1720s, The Rijksmuseum, Amsterdam, No. 2319
47 *Life and Letters of Mrs Delany*, 1st Series, Vol II, p 27, 23 Jan. 1738–9, ed Lady Llanover
48 FELKIN, op.cit. p 86
49 HENSON, op.cit. p 257 and FELKIN, op.cit. p 86
50 HENSON, op.cit. p 167
51 FELKIN, op.cit. p 86
52 DUNLEVY, op.cit. p 109
53 CUNNINGTON, op.cit. p 82
54 *The Leeds Mercury*, No. 568, 30 Nov. 1736. I am indebted here to Nicholas Brewster and Avril Hart
55 *The Universal Spectator*, quoted in CUNNINGTON, op.cit. p 174

56 *Receipt for Modern Dress*, quoted in Fairholt, op.cit. p 304
57 Accession No. 1953.312
58 *Pilborough's Colchester Journal*, quoted in Cunnington, op.cit. p 175
59 Bill quoted in N Waugh, op.cit. pp 99–100
60 For instance on p 17 of the *Master of the Robes accounts for year ended 13th February 1689*, LC9/389, Public Record Office. I am indebted here to Joanna Marschner
61 *Barbara Johnson's Albums of Fashions and Fabrics*, ed N Rothstein, Thames and Hudson, 1987, pp 161–5
62 New American Library edition, ch 7, pp 51–2; ch 36, p 232; ch 44, p 283; ch 3, p 29
63 Penguin edition, Vol I, *Letter 7*, p 50; Vol 1, *Letter 20*, p 77; Vol II, *The Journal*, pp 336–7
64 G Scott Thomson, *The Russells in Bloomsbury, 1669–1771*, Jonathan Cape, 1940, pp 274–5
65 S D Chapman, 'Genesis of the British Hosiery Industry, 1600–1750', *Textile History*, Vol 3, 1972, pp 21, 41

Chapter 3
1 W Gardiner, *Music and Friends*, 1838, Vol I, pp 43–4, 47
2 G Henson, *History of the Framework Knitters*, 1831, David & Charles, 1970, pp 171–3
3 *Reynolds*, ed N Penny, Royal Academy Exhibition catalogue, London, 1986, pp 181–3
4 Accession No. T439-1988
5 Henson, op.cit. pp 258–9
6 W Felkin, *History of the Machine-wrought Hosiery and Lace Manufactures*, Longmans, Green & Co, 1867, pp 90–3
7 Henson, op.cit. pp 273–5
8 Ibid. p 276
9 Felkin, op.cit. p 108
10 Ibid. p 110
11 Gardiner, op.cit. p 31
12 Felkin, op.cit. pp 110–11
13 Henson, op.cit. p 343
14 B du Mortier, 'Men's Fashion in the Netherlands, 1790–1830', *Costume 22*, 1988, pp 57–8
15 Henson, op.cit. p 345
16 Felkin, op.cit. p 113
17 Henson, op.cit. p 356
18 Ibid. p 353
19 For Boilly see F Boucher, *A History of Costume in the West*, Thames & Hudson, 1967, p 337; For Vernet see A Ribeiro, *Fashion in the French Revolution*, Batsford, 1988, p 116
20 Accession No. 4-34
21 N Waugh, *The Cut of Men's Clothes, 1600–1900*, Faber & Faber, 1964, p 107

22 Oct. 1772, quoted in *The Lady's Realm*, Jan. 1899, pp 359–60
23 Gardiner, op.cit. Vol III, 1853, p 129
24 Felkin, op.cit. p 113
25 Accession No. T1723-1913
26 F A Pottle, *Boswell's London Journal, 1762–3*, Penguin, 1966, p 257
27 Accession No. NCM 1985.770/30
28 A Ribeiro, *Dress and Morality*, Batsford, 1986, p 114; and *Fashion in the French Revolution*, Batsford, 1988, plate 71
29 Henson, op.cit. pp 290, 352
30 See Felkin, op.cit. p 102–7 for openwork
31 Henson, op.cit. p 416
32 Ibid. p 417; Felkin, op.cit. p 434
33 Public Record Office, LC9/389, *Master of the Robes accounts for the year ended 13th February 1689*, p 25
34 Ibid. p 29. I am indebted here to J Marschner
35 *The Journeys of Celia Fiennes*, ed C Morris, Cresset Press, 1949, p 234
36 T Rath, 'The Tewkesbury Hosiery Industry', *Textile History*, Vol 7, 1976, p 141
37 Ibid. p 143
38 Felkin, op.cit. p 76
39 Henson, op.cit. pp 360–3
40 Rath, op.cit. p 149
41 See W English, 'A Technical Assessment of Lewis Paul's Spinning Machine', *Textile History*, Vol 4, 1973, pp 68–83
42 Henson, op.cit. pp 365–6
43 Ibid. p 368
44 Felkin, op.cit. p 96
45 Museum of Costume and Textiles, Nottingham, accession Nos NCM 1985.770/2,3,4,8
46 Felkin, op.cit. p 120; *Great Exhibition catalogue*, Vol II, p 583; *Catalogue of the Exhibition of Arts, Manufactures [etc] at the Exchange Rooms, Nottingham*, 1840, p 60
47 National Portrait Gallery, London, No. 5101
48 Captain Jesse, *The Life of George Brummell Esq*, 1886, Vol I, p 62
49 Gardiner, op.cit. Vol I, 1838, p 265
50 Ibid. Vol III, 1853, p 283
51 M Dunlevy, *Dress in Ireland*, Batsford, 1989, p 109
52 *London Magazine*, in F W Fairholt, *Costume in England*, second edition, 1860, p 310
53 Anon, *History of British Costume*, Charles Knight, 1834, p 324
54 *Middleton Papers*, University of Nottingham, Mi, Av. 104/3, 102/10
55 Quoted in A Buck, *Dress in Eighteenth Century England*, Batsford, 1979, p 58
56 Quoted in *The Ladies' Penny Gazette*, December 7, 1833, p 40
57 du Mortier, op.cit. p 56

58 C P Moritz, *The Travels of Carl Philip Moritz in England in 1782*, quoted in A Buck, op.cit. p 92; M Ghering van Ierlant, 'Anglo-French Fashion 1786', *Costume* 17, 1983, p 69

59 J MacDonald, *Memoirs of an Eighteenth Century Footman*, Century Publishing, 1985, p 82

60 Buck, op.cit. p 138

61 *The Housekeeping Book of Susannah Whatman*, 1776, Century Publishing and the National Trust, 1987, pp 38, 50

62 P Hayden, 'Record of the Clothing Expenditure 1746–79, kept by Elizabeth Jervis', *Costume* 2, 1988, p 38

63 S Bamford, *Tawk o' Searth Lankeshur*, 1850, pp 7, 10, quoted in Buck, op.cit. p 149

64 G Scott Thomson, *The Russells in Bloomsbury, 1669–1771*, Jonathan Cape, 1940, p 229

65 F Burney, *Cecilia*, 1782, Book II, ch 1

66 Buck, op.cit. pp 134, 179; also pp 147–51 for following refs to worsted hose

67 C W & P Cunnington, *A Handbook of English Costume in the Eighteenth Century*, Faber & Faber, 1957, p 396

68 Dunlevy, op.cit. pp 129–130

69 Felkin, op.cit. p 434

70 See G. Grull, 'The Poneggen Hosiery Enterprise, 1763–1818', *Textile History*, Vol 5, 1975, pp 38–79

71 I Barnes, 'The Aberdeen Stocking Trade', *Textile History*, Vol 8, 1977, pp 90–1

72 R Campbell, *The London Tradesman*, London, 1747, p 215

73 M Sonenscher, 'The Hosiery Industry of Nîmes and the Lower Languedoc in the Eighteenth Century', *Textile History*, Vol 10, 1976, p 154

74 C Heywood, 'The Rural Hosiery Industry of the Lower Champagne Region, 1750–1850', *Textile History*, Vol 7, 1976, pp 90–111

75 M Grass, *A History of Hosiery*, Fairchild Publications, 1955, ch 14, pp 171–189

76 Buck, op.cit. pp 95–6

Chapter 4

1 J Blackner, *The History of Nottingham...*, Nottingham, 1815, pp 238–40; W Felkin, *An Account of the machine-wrought Hosiery Trade...*, W Strange, 1845, pp 7–16

2 Felkin, op.cit. pp 28–9, 34–5; W Felkin, *History of the Machine-wrought Hosiery and Lace Manufactures*, Longmans, Green & Co, 1867, p 458

3 Felkin, *History*, op.cit. p 231

4 See F M Thomas, *I & R Morley, A Record of a Hundred Years*, Chiswick Press, 1900

5 As Ward, Sharp & Co in 1801, N B Harte, 'The Growth and Decay of a Hosiery Firm in

the Nineteenth Century', *Textile History*, Vol 8, 1977, p 8

6 See K Jopp, *Corah of Leicester, 1815–1965*, 1965

7 G Ekstrand, 'Some Early Silk Stockings in Sweden', *Textile History*, Vol 13 (2), 1982, pp 174, 176

8 Felkin, *History*, op.cit. p 82

9 *Salisbury Journal*, quoted in C W & P Cunnington, *A Handbook of English Costume in the Eighteenth Century*, Faber & Faber, 1957, p 396; W Gardiner, *Music and Friends*, Vol I, 1838, p 362

10 G Grull, 'The Ponnegen Hosiery Enterprise', *Textile History*, Vol 5, 1974, p 70

11 Felkin, *History*, op.cit. p 237

12 *The Times*, 1799, quoted in C W & P Cunnington, *The History of Underclothes*, Michael Joseph, 1951, p 108

13 *Chester Chronicle*, quoted in C W & P Cunnington, *English Women's Clothing in the Nineteenth Century*, Faber & Faber, 1937, p 368

14 *La Belle Assemblée*, April 1812, p 22

15 Ibid. August 1811, p 2; February 1812, p 13

16 *Selected Letters of Jane Austen*, ed R W Chapman, World Classics, 1955, p 110

17 *La Belle Assemblée*, December 1811, p 43; April 1812, p 22

18 Ibid. February 1812, p 12

19 M B Harvey, *A Journal of a Voyage from Philadelphia to Cork in the year of Our Lord, 1809*, Philadelphia, 1915, p 31, quoted in M Dunlevy, *Dress in Ireland*, Batsford, 1989, p 131

20 Cunnington, *English Womens' Clothing...*, op.cit. p 39

21 Felkin, *History*, op.cit. p 168

22 Ibid. pp 300–303

23 *La Belle Assemblée*, January 1815, p 38

24 Cunnington, op.cit. p 83

25 *The World of Fashion*, Sep. 1827, p 202; March 1828, p 60

26 Ibid. April 1829, p 84

27 Ibid. December 1829, p 228

28 *The World of Fashion*, pp 36, 60, 84, 108

29 Ibid. October 1829, p 228

30 Cunnington, op.cit. p 116

31 *The World of Fashion*, p 252, and *The Lady's Magazine and Museum*, July 1835, p 59

32 *The World of Fashion*, September 1825, p 318

33 Accession No. 1947-3414

34 Accession No. NCM 1985.770/6

35 Accession No. 1977-504

36 Anonymous caricature, *The Separation, a sketch from the private life of Lord Iron*. Published by J Sidebotham, No. 96, Strand [London]

37 Cunnington, op.cit. p 116

38 Felkin, *History*, op.cit. p 493
39 *Great Exhibition Catalogue*, 1851, Vol II, p 576
40 Accession Nos NCM 1985.770/11, 17
41 Felkin, *History*, op.cit. pp 492–3
42 C Dickens, *Sketches by Boz*, 1836–7, Characters, ch IV, Miss Evans and the Eagle; Tales, The Boarding-House, ch 2
43 Mayhew Brothers, *The Greatest Plague of Life, or the Adventures of a Lady in Search of a Good Servant*, David Bogue, 1847, p 87
44 *The World of Fashion*, June 1829, p 138
45 Quoted in Harte, op.cit. pp 38–9
46 Mayhew Brothers, op.cit. p 210
47 R Rutt, *A History of Hand Knitting*, Batsford, 1987, pp 111–7
48 Accession Nos 1940.119/2, 1953.44
49 Quoted in Harte, op.cit. p 39
50 Gardiner, op.cit. Vol III, 1853, pp 31–2
51 Captain Jesse, *The Life of George Brummell Esq*, 1886, Vol I, p 63
52 *The Reminiscences and Recollections of Captain Gronow*, ed J Raymond, Bodley Head, 1964, p 191
53 T Dyche and W Pardon, *A New General English Dictionary*, 1758
54 C Dickens, *Sketches by Boz*, 1836–7, 'The Couple who coddle themselves'
55 Portrait of John Keats, National Portrait Gallery, London, No. 58; portrait of Baron Schwiter, National Gallery, London, No. 3286
56 *The World of Fashion*, September 1826, p 299
57 C Dickens, *The Pickwick Club*, 1836–7, ch 41, ch 27
58 C Dickens, *Sketches by Boz*, 1836–7, 'The Bloomsbury Christening'
59 Examples in Northampton Museum, illustrated in J Swann, *Shoes*, Batsford, 1982, p 43, and, dated 1842, in the Museum of Costume and Textiles, Nottingham, NCM 1966.12
60 C Dickens, *The Pickwick Club*, 1836–7, ch 28
61 *The World of Fashion*, June 1826, p 215
62 C Dickens, *The Pickwick Club*, 1836–7, ch 35
63 Letter at the Ruddington Framework Knitters Museum
64 R S Surtees, *Mr Sponge's Sporting Tour*, 1853, p 110
65 Gardiner, op.cit. Vol I, 1838, pp 467–8
66 *The World of Fashion*, March 1826, p 107
67 A G Osler, 'Tyneside Riverworkers: Occupational Dress', *Costume* 18, 1984, p 74
68 See G Borrow, *Wild Wales*, 1862
69 M Hartley and J Iingilby, *The Old Hand-knitters of the Dales*, Dalesman Publishing, 1969, p 30
70 *Middleton Papers*, University of Nottingham, Mi.Av.121/1
71 Accession Nos T57-1959, T59-1959
72 *Industries of Dublin, c* 1883, p 78, information kindly supplied by Mairead Dunlevy
73 *Report of the Juries of the Great Exhibition*, 1852, class 20, p 477

Chapter 5

1 W Gardiner, *Music and Friends*, 1838, Vol II, p 571
2 W Felkin, *An Account of the Machine-Wrought Hosiery Trade . . .*, W Strange, 1845, p 9
3 W Felkin, *History of the Machine-Wrought and Lace Manufactures*, Longmans, Green & Co, 1867, pp 489–490
4 M Dubuisson, *Le Musée de la Bonneterie, Troyes*, in *La Vie en Champagne*, September 1974, pp 12–14
5 Felkin, *History*, op.cit. p 505
6 A Nutting, *Salient Features of Knitting Technology*, in *Four Centuries of Machine Knitting*, ed J Millington and S Chapman, Knitting International, Leicester, 1989, p 58
7 Felkin, *History*, op.cit. pp 496–502
8 M N Grass *A History of Hosiery*, Fairchild Publications, USA, 1955, p 197
9 Ibid. p 207
10 Ibid. p 220
11 *The Queen*, 7 March, 1873, p 163
12 *The Englishwoman's Domestic Magazine*, February 1870, p 107
13 Grass, op.cit. p 210
14 W H Wylie, *Old and New Nottingham*, London 1853, p 299; the factory was built in 1851
15 N B Harte, 'The Growth and Decay of a Hosiery Firm in the 19th Century', *Textile History*, Vol 8, 1977, p 42
16 F M Thomas, *I & R Morley, A Record of a Hundred Years*, Chiswick Press, 1900, p 31; and K Jopp, *Corah of Leicester, 1815–1965*, Leicester 1965, pp 11–12
17 Thomas, op.cit. for this and most information about I & R Morley
18 *Nottingham Guardian*, 15 May, 1948
19 Article in *The Derbyshire Advertiser*, 10 March 1911, also photograph and letter from Swears & Wells at Derby Museum
20 F Dimond and R Taylor, *Crown and Camera*, Penguin Books, 1987, p 182
21 W Felkin, *Hosiery and Lace*, in *British Manufacturing Industries*, ed G Bevan, E Stanford, 1876, pp 42–3
22 *The Queen*, 23 November 1872, p 428
23 M Dunlevy, *Dress in Ireland*, Batsford, 1989, p 158
24 *The Girls' Own Paper*, 3 February 1883, p 287
25 Ibid. 11 October 1890, p 31
26 *The Milliner and Dressmaker*, June 1875, p 21
27 and 28 *The Englishwoman's Domestic Magazine*, Aug. 1863, p 189

29 Ibid. December 1860, p 93
30 *The Queen*, 3 August 1872, p 86
31 *The Milliner and Dressmaker*, May 1875, p 24
32 *Cassells' Family Magazine*, Sept. 1878, p 634
33 *The Girls' Own Paper*, 23 Feb. 1884, p 329
34 Ibid. 26 April 1884, p 474
35 *The Young Ladies' Journal*, Dec. 1890, p 346
36 *Vanity Fair*, 18 June 1914
37 Made by Pope & Plante, *Illustrated London News*, 6 May 1843
38 *The Queen*, 29 March 1873, p 253
39 *The Ladies' Treasury*, August 1877, p 475
40 *The Ladies' Field*, 12 April 1914, p 352
41 Lawrence's wife, Frieda, is noted as wearing 'grass-green' stockings in *c* 1916
42 *The Lady's Realm*, March 1899, p 621
43 THOMAS, op.cit. p 41
44 S D CHAPMAN, 'Enterprise and Innovation in the British Hosiery Industry, 1750–1850', *Textile History*, Vol 5, 1974, p 21
45 THOMAS, op.cit. pp 41–2; also R FINCH, *The Flying Wheel, I & R Morley, c* 1920, pp 24–5
46 E.g., in *The Sketch*, 5 Feb. 1919, p III
47 *The Girls' Own Paper*, 28 Aug. 1897, pp 761–2
48 Z SCHONFIELD, 'Miss Marshall and the Cimabue Browns', *Costume* 13, 1979, p 71
49 L HAMER, 'The Cullercoats Fishwife', *Costume* 18, 1984, p 70
50 By Madame Bergman Osterberg, a Swedish teacher at Dartford College for Physical Training. It was widely adopted. See E EWING, *History of Children's Costume*, Bibliophile, London 1977, p 123 and P CUNNINGTON and A MANSFIELD, *English Costume for Sports and Outdoor Recreation*, A & C Black, 1969, p 45
51 C V BALSAN, *The Glitter and the Gold*, Heinemann, 1953, pp 20–1
52 LOELIA, DUCHESS OF WESTMINSTER, *Grace and Favour*, Weidenfeld & Nicolson, 1961, p 62
53 *The Young Ladies' Journal*, 1874, Vol XI, No. 529, p 410
54 *The Girls' Own Paper*, 28 August 1897, p 762
55 *The Lady's Realm*, Vol 37, Sept. 1915, p 350
56 *The Englishwoman's Domestic Magazine*, July 1862, p 142
57 *The Milliner and Dressmaker*, January 1880, p 6
58 *The Lady's Pictorial*, 3 August 1889, p 171
59 Accession No. 589-1962; mark 'A' for Allen, Solly & Co of Nottingham
60 *The Milliner and Dressmaker*, June 1879, p 17
61 *La Nouvelle Mode*, 7 October 1911, p 10
62 Accession No. T589-1962, illustrated in *Four Hundred Years of Fashion*, ed N ROTHSTEIN, Victoria and Albert Museum and William Collins, 1984, p 114
63 *The Ladies' Field*, 6 April 1912, p 257
64 *The Milliner and Dressmaker*, April 1879, p 15
65 *The Girls' Own Paper*, 4 May 1889, p 495
66 *The Queen*, 14 Dec. 1872, p 487; 4 Jan. 1873, p 17
67 *The Milliner and Dressmaker*, June 1875, p 17
68 THOMAS, op.cit. pp 36–7
69 *The Girls' Own Paper*, 22 April 1882, p 472
70 Accession Nos 83.672/19 (London) and NCM 1975.162. (Nottingham).
71 *The Girls' Own Paper*, 26 August 1893, p 761
72 National Portrait Gallery Nos 3116 and 4584
73 A jocular variant of 'nut', in use 1911 to 1919 for a dandified young man, see popular song of 1915 by A WIMPERIS *Gilbert the Filbert, the Colonel of the Knuts*
74 *Daily Mirror*, 1914; from an album of press cuttings in the Fashion Research Centre, Bath
75 ANON, *Etiquette of Good Society*, Cassell, Peter Galphin & Co, *c* 1880, p 87
76 *The Englishwoman's Domestic Magazine*, July 1870, p 30
77 *The Queen*, 19 October 1872, p 309
78 *The Tailor and Cutter*, 1 Dec. 1893, pp 367–8
79 R S SURTEES, *Mr Sponge's Sporting Tour*, 1853, ch 24
80 *The Englishwoman's Domestic Magazine*, September 1870, p 178
81 *The Girls' Own Paper*, 31 Dec. 1898, p 218
82 *The Englishwoman's Domestic Magazine*, April and May 1871, pp 239, 302
83 THE DUKE OF WINDSOR, *A Family Album*, Cassell, 1960, pp 24–7
84 *The Milliner and Dressmaker*, Jan. 1879, p 17
85 Patent No. 2081, 29 May 1877
86 *The Milliner and Dressmaker*, Dec. 1875, p 24
87 *The Girls' Own Paper*, 7 October 1893, p 13
88 Ibid. 29 November 1884, p 138, and 21 March 1891, p 399
89 *The Young Englishwoman*, July 1876, p 416
90 *The Girls' Own Paper*, 28 Aug. 1897, pp 761–2
91 From an album of press cuttings, Fashion Research Centre, Bath
92 D R GOADBY, *Fully-fashioned to Seamless; Productivity and Fashion*, in *Four Centuries of Machine Knitting*, ed J MILLINGTON and S D CHAPMAN, Knitting International, Leicester, 1989, p 166

Chapter 6

1 C W CUNNINGTON, *Englishwomen's Costume in the Present Century*, Faber & Faber, 1952, p 168
2 Accession No. NCM 1986.1092
3 The London Glove Co Ltd, and The London Hole-proof Hosiery Co in *The Queen*, 20 November 1920
4 LOELIA, DUCHESS OF WESTMINSTER, *Grace and Favour*, Weidenfeld and Nicolson, 1961, p 96

5   *The Tatler*, 30 July 1924, p ii, and ibid.
    17 February 1926 p ii
6   Ibid. 4 November 1925, p 244
7   Ibid. 30 July 1924, p ii
8   Ibid. 17 February 1926, p ii
9   Ibid. 27 January 1926, p 184
10 Ibid. 4 November 1925, p iii
11 D C COLEMAN, *A Brief History of Courtaulds*,
    1969, p 11
12 Ibid. p 14
13 *Threads, the Magazine of I & R Morley*, July
    1927, pp 10–11
14 Brand names of F Ellis & Co of Leicester and
    Wardle and Davenport Ltd of Leek
15 Brand name of Johnson and Barnes Ltd of
    Leicester
16 *The Tatler*, 3 February 1926, p 230
17 Advertisement in *The Gentlewoman*, 1924–5
18 Made by Leo Ltd of Mansfield
19 A LANSDELL, 'Costume for Oarswomen, 1919–
    1979', *Costume* 13, 1979, pp 74–75
20 THE DUKE OF WINDSOR, *A Family Album*, Cassell,
    1960, p 130
21 B BURMAN and M LEVENTON, 'The Men's Dress
    Reform Party, 1929–1937', *Costume* 21,
    1987, p 80
22 *Simpson's Magazine for Men*, Spring 1937
23 Made by Stephens Brothers (who traded as
    Tenova Ltd in the 1930s and are now a
    subsidiary of Austin Reed). They hold the royal
    warrants of appointment to the Prince of
    Wales and the Duke of Edinburgh
24 *Harper's Bazaar*, June 1935
25 Army & Navy Stores, *Catalogue 1933–4* p 702
26 A W ELEY, *Stockings*, Hosiery Trade Journal,
    Leicester, 1953, p 217
27 and 28   *Harper's Bazaar*, April 1935, p 140
29 Advertisement for Ballito, *Woman's Journal*,
    May 1938, p 103
30 M GRASS, *A History of Hosiery*, Fairchild
    Publications, 1955, p 263
31 K JOPP, *Corah of Leicester, 1815–1965*, 1965,
    p 33
32 Perhaps similar to the 'Renewable Stockings'
    in The *Englishwoman's Domestic Magazine*,
    November 1860, p 46
33 *Housewife*, January 1947, p 40
34 Advertisement for Taylor-Woods nylons in
    Woman's Journal, December 1953, p 9
35 ELEY, op.cit. p 207
36 GRASS, op.cit. p 252
37 HATRA press release, 30 October 1952
38 *Housewife*, January 1947, p 40
39 D R GOADBY, *Fully-fashioned to seamless;
    productivity and Fashion*, in *Four Centuries of
    Machine Knitting*, ed J MILLINGTON and S D
    CHAPMAN, Knitting International, Leicester,
    1989, p 166

Chapter 7

1   E CARTER, *The Changing World of Fashion*,
    Weidenfeld & Nicolson, 1977, p 212
2   *Vogue*, Jan. 1965, p 59; ibid. Sept. 1967,
    p 121
3   G S BEATTIE, *The History of Pretty Polly, 1919–
    79* (unpublished), pp 59–60
4   *Vogue*, May 1966, p 154
5   Advertisement, *Sunday Times*, 13 Oct. 1968
6   CARTER, op.cit. p 206
7   Ibid. p 205
8   Ibid. p 213
9   *Nottingham Evening Post*, 8 Nov. 1977, p 4
10 *Harper's & Queen*, September 1976, p 180
11 *Woman's Journal*, January 1977, p 15
12 *Cosmopolitan*, September 1978, p 138
13 *Nottingham Evening Post*, 15 March 1977, p 15
14 S TURNER, *The History of Pretty Polly, the 1980s*,
    (unpublished) p 9
15 *Nottingham Evening Post*, 12 September 1980,
    p 12, and 13 April 1982, p 6
16 Ibid. 16 September 1988, p 10
17 S TURNER, op.cit. p 41
18 *The Sunday Times*, 4 May 1983, p 8
19 S TURNER, op.cit. p 29
20 *Telegraph Sunday Magazine*, 23 Nov. 1986,
    p 51
21 Ibid. 25 August 1985, p 27
22 N COHN, *Today There Are No Gentlemen*,
    Weidenfeld & Nicolson, 1971, p 29
23 *Style*, December 1971, p 26
24 Ibid. March 1972, p 34
25 Accession Nos T349-1984, T318-1985,
    T317-1985
26 THE DUKE OF WINDSOR, *A Family Album*, Cassell,
    1960, p 119
27 and 28   C HIX, *Dressing Right*, St Martin's Press,
    New York, 1978, p 168
29 *Weldon's Ladies' Journal*, May 1914, p xxi and
    p xxxviii
30 *The Sketch*, 4 December 1918, p e
31 *Nottingham Evening Post*, 12 Sept. 1980, p 12
32 Ibid. 2 November 1990, p 14
33 'Legs Take a New Fashion Stance', *Du Pont
    Magazine*, European edition, No. 4, 1982

Glossary

Aesthetic movement   English art movement of the 1870s and 1880s, an amalgam of elements from Classical, Japanese and Dutch traditions combined with an observation of nature. In dress expressed in drapery on the naturally contoured body without the artificial aids of corsets or bustles.

Argyles   socks or stockings with a tartan pattern; said to have been invented in the 1890s.

Aulnage   the official inspection, measurement and valuation of woollen cloth for excise duty.

Balbriggan   good quality hose made from Sea Island cotton, of seven or nine threads twisted together. Named after a village north of Dublin, but used for any high quality hose of this type.

Balzarine   a dress material of cotton and worsted fashionable in the 1830s and 1840s.

Beaver   yarn spun from the under-fur of the European rodent (Castor fiber) or its North American cousin (Castor canadensis). Prized for its warmth. Elizabeth Charlotte, Duchess of Orleans, mentioned donning beaver stockings on 6 November 1721. Beaver stockings were also shown at the Great Exhibition in 1851.

Bemberg   rayon made by the cuprammonium process. Bemberg chiffonella was described as the wonder yarn of the century in the late 1930s.

Bump   Westmorland and Yorkshire dialect for very coarse wool or yarn.

Cashmere   the hair from the undercoat of the Kashmir goat woven into soft fabric; in hosiery in the nineteenth and twentieth centuries cashmere meant sheep's wool. Recently tights have been made of the real cashmere.

Casimir   or kerseymere; a soft woollen cloth of twill weave used for clothes and furnishing; patented by Francis Yerbury of Bradford in 1766.

Chevening   1780s into the 20th century; from the Anglo-Saxon 'to finish', fine embroidery on machine knitted hose.

Circular machine   a knitting machine in which the needles are in a ring rather than in a row.

Clock   vertical embroidered or knitted decoration over the ankle bone; said to be because of similarity to a clock pendulum, but origin obscure.

Compenzine   silk thread of two or more highly twisted threads combined with an untwisted thread.

and then reverse twisted, making a tight, hard and smooth thread.

Cothurne   from *cothurnus*, a thick-soled boot reaching to the upper calf, worn by tragic actors in ancient Athenian drama. The word was used again in revivals of classical dress in the late eighteenth century and in about 1912, when it referred to a shoe tied onto the foot by ribbon straps crossing up the leg, as such it was synonymous with the 'tango' shoe.

Course or row   a horizontal line of loops in knitting.

Cradle sole   a narrow strip of thicker thread linking the thicker thread reinforcements at toe and heel.

Crepe   a combination of two threads, each twisted in the opposite direction, and bound together with a slight binding twist, creating a matt but elastic thread.

Cut-ups   stockings or socks cut from yardage machine knitting, rather than shaped on the machine.

Denier   an Italian weight standardised as 0.05 grams. The weight in deniers of 450 metres of thread determines the denier rating of the thread.

English foot   hose with a separately made sole seamed in along the sides of the foot.

Fashioned or fully fashioned   stocking or sock or indeed any garment shaped on the knitting machine by either increasing or decreasing the number of loops per row.

French foot   hose with a seam under the foot; worn particularly with low-cut shoes.

Gabrielle style   from 1865, a style of female dress cut without a waist seam, with the weight of the dress hanging from the shoulders. Adopted first by the dress reform movements and then generally for girls' dress.

Garnsey/guernsey   worsted thread from long staple wool, spun on the small Guernsey wheel.

Gauge   originally the number of needles per inch on the stocking frame; but from the early 19th century the number of needles per one and a half inches. Therefore 48 gauge equals 32 needles per inch; circular machine gauge is measured by the number of needles in the ring.

Ghillie shoes   walking shoes for both sexes and originally from Scotland; the laces criss-cross over the instep through loops, instead of holes, each side of the opening, and are tied above the ankle bone.

Gore clock triangular piece or gore let in at the ankle of a stocking; often made in one piece with the stocking sole.

Intarsia knitting technique in which two areas of different colour are linked by twisting the threads of both colours together where they join, rather than taking the threads of one colour across the back of the other.

Kersey coarse woollen cloth of twill weave, named after the town in Suffolk; very resistant to cold and wet and much used for cloth stockings.

Lace clock at the ankle of hose, decoration which is formed of holes rather than embroidered.

Ladder stop a band of holes or fancy mesh at the top or toe of a stocking to prevent a ladder going right to the edge of the stocking.

Lastex rubber thread made from extruded latex, rather than cut from strips of cured latex.

Lisle originally a linen thread from Lille in France; in hosiery two-ply cotton yarn with the two plies twisted in opposite directions and then twisted together, often gassed. Makes a hard, resilient thread.

Marl perhaps a contraction of 'marline', a small line of two strands, or perhaps of 'marbled'; thread of two or more strands of different colours twisted together, giving a speckled appearance.

Mercerisation method of imparting a gloss to cotton thread by passing it under tension through a caustic soda solution.

Merino in hosiery, a thread of cotton and wool.

Milanese from c 1900, a warp knitted silk in which the threads instead of looping in vertical zigzags, loop diagonally, making a more flexible fabric. Usually more expensive than ordinary stockings as made of thinner silk but they did not ladder. Superseded with other silk stockings by nylons in the later 1950s.

Ombre yarns, fabrics and garments, being of one colour but shaded from pale to dark.

Organzine raw silk threads twisted in one direction 14 to 16 times, doubled, and given a reverse twist 12 times. Makes a strong, elastic thread.

Picot edge row of holes in the welt, which, when folded over, makes an edging of tiny loops or arches at the top of the welt.

Plating using one thread on top of another so that hose is of one fibre on the face and another on the reverse.

Point heel heel reinforcement shaped to a point at the back.

Quirk a sixteenth century term for 'clock'.

Sandals nineteenth century, ribbons or tapes which criss-cross over the instep and lower leg holding the low-cut shoe in place.

Scotch thread cf Lisle

Sea Island cotton soft, silky cotton from the islands off Georgia and South Carolina, USA. Production ceased after the plantations were destroyed by the cotton-boll weevil in the 1960s.

Seamless/seam free hose made on circular knitting machines, and with neither real nor simulated back seams.

Serge twilled weave worsted cloth.

Shadow welt/after welt 1930s onwards, the band between the welt and the leg of the stocking.

Shoe rose late sixteenth and seventeenth centuries; ornamental rosette concealing shoe fastening.

Shot ribbed hosiery with the ribs on the face of a different colour from those on the reverse; when stretched the two colours appear together.

Space-dyed threads tied tightly at intervals before dyeing so that only the areas between the ties are dyed, creating a parti-coloured appearance.

Stockinet machine knitted fabric.

Thread in the seventeenth and eighteenth centuries often meant a linen thread; in the nineteenth century often a Lisle thread.

Tickler small piece of metal with a groove at the top and another at the bottom, made to fit over the head of the needle in the stocking frame to enable stitches to be transferred from one needle to another without forming ladders.

Turn shapes pattern made of frame knitted stockings by twisting loops; the framework equivalent of purl stitch.

Wales vertical columns of stitches.

Weaving/woven with regard to hosiery often meaning machine knitted.

Welt the top or hem at the stocking top, made of a double layer of machine knitting.

Museums to visit

Gallery of English Costume, Platt Hall, Rusholme, Manchester
Killerton House, Broadclyst, Exeter, Devon
Leicestershire Museums, Art Galleries and Records Service, 9 New Walk, Leicester
Municipal Museum, Civic Centre, Mount Pleasant, Tunbridge Wells, Kent
Museum of Costume, Bath Museums Service, 4 The Circus, Bath, Avon
Museum of Costume and Textiles, 51 Castle Gate, Nottingham
Museum of London, London Wall, London EC2
National Museums of Scotland, Chambers Street, Edinburgh
Pickford's House Museum, 41 Friar Gate, Derby
Victoria and Albert Museum, Cromwell Road, South Kensington, London SW7
Weybridge Museum, Church Street, Weybridge, Surrey
York Castle Museum, York

These museums house the largest collections of stockings and socks, but any museum with a costume collection will probably have some women's stockings; men's socks, like much men's clothing, are harder to find. *A Handbook of Costume* by Janet Arnold (Macmillan 1973) is still a useful guide to costume museums and collections.

Select Bibliography

BLUM, S, *Victorian Fashions and Costumes from Harper's Bazaar, 1867–8*, Dover 1974
BRADFIELD, N, *Costume in detail*, Harrap 1968
BUCK, A, *Dress in Eighteenth Century England*, Batsford 1979
   Victorian Costume and Costume Accessories, Herbert Jenkins 1961
CHAPMAN, S D, 'The Genesis of the British Hosiery Trade', *Textile History*, Vol 3, 1972
CHAPMAN, S D, 'Enterprise and Innovation in the British Hosiery Industry, 1750–1850', *Textile History*, Vol 5, 1974
CROFT, P, 'The Rise of the English Stocking Trade', *Textile History*, Vol 18, No. 1, Spring 1987
CUNNINGTON, C W, *English Women's Clothing in the Nineteenth Century*, Faber 1937
English Women's Clothing in the Present Century, Faber 1952
CUNNINGTON, C W & P, *A Handbook of English Costume in the Sixteenth Century*, Faber 1954
   A Handbook of English Costume in the Seventeenth Century, Faber 1955
   A Handbook of English Costume in the Eighteenth Century, Faber 1957
   A Handbook of English Costume in the Nineteenth Century, Faber 1959, 1970
EKSTRAND, G, 'Some Early Silk Stockings in Sweden', *Textile History*, Vol 13, No. 2, Autumn 1982
ELEY, A W, *Stockings*, Hosiery Trade Journal Ltd, 1953
FELKIN W, *A History of the Machine Wrought Hosiery and Lace Manufactures*, 1867, reprinted with introduction by S D Chapman, David & Charles 1967
GRASS M N, *A History of Hosiery*, Fairchild Publications Inc 1955
GRASS M N, *Stockings for a Queen*, 1967
HENSON, G, *A History of the Framework Knitters*, 1831, reprinted with introduction by S D CHAPMAN, David & Charles 1967
LEVEY S M, 'Illustrations of the History of Knitting Selected from the Collection of the Victoria and Albert Museum', *Textile History*, Vol 1, No. 2, 1969
LEWIS, P, 'William Lee's Stocking Frame: Technical Evolution and Economic Viability, 1589–1750', *Textile History*, Vol 17, No. 2, Autumn 1986
MILLINGTON, J T & CHAPMAN S D, eds *Four Centuries of Machine Knitting, commemorating William Lee's Invention of the Stocking Frame in 1589*, Knitting International, Vol 96, Feb 1989
PASOLD E W, 'In Search of William Lee', *Textile History*, Vol 6, 1975
RAPLEY J, 'Handframe Knitting: The Development of Patterning and Shaping', *Textile History*, Vol 6, 1975
RUTT, R, *A History of Hand Knitting*, Batsford, 1987
THIRSK J, 'The fantastical folly of fashion: the English Stocking Industry, 1500–1700', in HARTE N B and PONTING, K G, eds, *Textile History and Economic History; Essays in Honour of Miss Julia de Lacy Mann*, Manchester University Press 1973
WELLS F A, *The British Hosiery and Knitwear Industry*, 1935, revised edition, David & Charles 1972

An extensive bibliography on hosiery, compiled by Madeleine Ginsburg, was published in *Costume, the Journal of the Costume Society*, No. 2, 1968

Index

LIBRARY
ST. LOUIS COMMUNITY COLLEGE
AT FLORISSANT VALLEY